Self-Esteem F

Skyrocket Your Self Confidence, Charisma & Become The Alpha Male

© **Copyright 2020 by Darcy Carter - All rights reserved.**

The contents of this book may not be reproduced, duplicated, or transmitted without direct written permission from the author.

Under no circumstances will any legal responsibility or blame be held against the publisher for any reparation, damages, or monetary loss due to the information herein, either directly or indirectly.

Legal Notice:

This book is copyright protected. This is only for personal use. You cannot amend, distribute, sell, use, quote, or paraphrase any part of the content within this book without the consent of the author.

Disclaimer Notice:

Please note the information contained within this document is for educational and entertainment purposes only. Every attempt has been made to provide accurate, up to date, and reliable information. No warranties of any kind are expressed or implied. Readers acknowledge that the author is not engaging in the rendering of legal, financial, medical, or professional advice. The content of this book has been derived from various sources. Please consult a licensed professional before attempting any techniques outlined in this book.

By reading this document, the reader agrees that under no circumstances are the author responsible for any losses, direct or indirect, which are incurred as a result of the use of the information contained within this document, including, but not limited to, —errors, omissions, or inaccuracies.

The First 9 Things A Woman Notices

Free Cheat Sheet For Attracting Women

Click Here

Click Here

THE FIRST 9 THINGS A WOMAN NOTICES 3

CLICK HERE 3

INTRODUCTION 6

UNDERSTANDING SELF-ESTEEM AND CONFIDENCE 12

Self-esteem 12

Confidence 13

What are the causes of low self-esteem and confidence? 16

Human motivation 28

Exercise 30

HOW DO YOU STOP NEGATIVE THOUGHTS? 31

Beliefs 32

Positive Thinking 37

Self-efficacy 40

Exercise 44

RETRAIN YOUR BRAIN TO REVERSE NEGATIVE THINKING 45

Language 46

Cognitive behavioral therapy 49

Goals 52

Exercise 56

THE SURPRISING TRUTH ABOUT BEING A MAN 57

Masculine Vulnerability   60

Learning to accept yourself   67

Exercise   69

THE MALE BODY IMAGE CRISIS   70

Superheroes   72

Managing body image issues   75

Performance anxiety and sexual dysfunction   76

Exercise   77

CONFIDENCE IN CONVERSATION AND SOCIALIZING   78

Social skills & better conversations   79

Eliminate the fear of rejection   82

Nervousness and Social Anxiety   86

Charisma   87

Exercise   90

WORK AND RELATIONSHIPS   91

Work   91

Assertiveness   97

Dating and positive relationships   98

Criticism (and how to respond to it)   100

Exercise   102

CONCLUSION- LIVE LIFE TO THE MAX!   103

THANKS FOR READING!	108
THE FIRST 9 THINGS A WOMAN NOTICES	108
CLICK HERE	109
RESOURCES	109

Introduction

Self esteem and confidence, the foundations of living your best life. They are the keys to unlocking what you truly desire in your life. Although they might appear to be the same, confidence and self-esteem are in fact not the same. Self-esteem in the simplest of terms is, "how much you like yourself" and it is a critical determinant of a healthy personality. Everyone needs a healthy level of self-esteem to achieve their goals and overcome any obstacles in life. Adults who have a healthy level of self-esteem are more motivated and likelier to overcome any challenges towards their goals. How much confidence you have is directly affected by your self-esteem. Confidence simply put, is about your belief in yourself, skills and abilities. In a nutshell it is having faith in yourself.

Studies have shown that your self-esteem will be at its highest in childhood. After adolescence it declines, then during adulthood it rises again and then declines in older age. Life experiences also contribute to these fluctuations. Maybe you feel good about your home and work life but your relationships are a worry.

Those with high self-esteem feel loved, worthy and valued in the world. Those with low self-esteem feel less of themselves. Sometimes they might appear to be confident but often it is merely a mask of their negative inner dialogue and issues. Masking the problem only makes things worse. Men are often the first ones to close themselves off to expressing how they feel and older generations are particularly notorious for this. When we are surrounded by similar individuals it breeds more of the same masking behaviours. Without addressing these mental health issues they will impact negatively on our self-esteem. Low self-esteem can reduce quality of life in many different ways which can all lead to a negative cycle of frustration. Here are some of the most common effects of a low self-esteem.

- Avoiding people or situations that otherwise may have been beneficial
- Fear of talking to other people
- False beliefs of being unattractive, unwanted or not enough
- Poor judgement
- Self loathing
- False beliefs that most people do not like you

One of the worst negative side effects of low self-esteem is avoidance. Avoidance is a powerful defense mechanism to dealing with situations where you might have anxiety or fear. Often it kicks into gear without your awareness. That can be really trivial everyday situations such as going to the supermarket or answering the phone. The problem compounds because the more people fall into unconscious avoidance habits the deeper the habits form. Ultimately it will make you less competent and increasingly doubtful of yourself. But why waste years of your life neglecting what you want?

For men self-esteem issues are one of the last things they want to talk about. False constructs are out there about what it means to be a man. Men are 'expected to look muscular, be tough and emotionally unattached. But most feel they don't match up and this breeds a culture of men keeping quiet about their feelings. As a result many men isolate themselves because they fear their weaknesses being revealed.

This is a growing issue in the modern world. Now more than ever with economic pressure, pandemics and uncertainity. Add to that all the so called perfect lives that are portrayed on social media. It can be easy to shift the blame for your situation and say because of the way you were treated is the reason for why you are who you are. But the truth is that blame will only take you so far. At a certain point you're going to need to step up and take responsibility for who you are. No one else will.

Henry David Thoreau - "The mass of men lead lives of quiet desperation".

Barely been anything has been written about addressing these issues. This book sets out to help. There are distinct ways to improve confidence and self esteem. Ones that will effectively reprogram the way you think about yourself which will ultimately enhance your self-esteem and confidence. All of that and much more are covered in this book.

My name is Darcy Carter. I am a bestselling author of books on confidence, dating and social skills. I am also a singer and owner of a distribution company. My knowledge comes from real life experience. It's tried and tested. You see I used to be someone who was afraid to go out of the house. I let my hair grow long, I didn't buy new clothes for years and I buried myself in work so that I didn't have to face the world out there. Neglect and avoidance caused me to miss out on valuable years of my life. Frustrated and at breaking point I decided to make drastic changes to my life. So I took a leap of faith and moved to another country where I was forced to take action. I had to meet new people and I had to become better. As a result I am now a more confident person than ever before and I have an exciting social life. I'm giving you all I know here plus more that I have researched, tested and discussed with other highly confident people.

In this book first of all I will give you a concrete understanding of self-esteem and confidence. Discover the causes of your low self-esteem and confidence. Maybe it was from your childhood, life experiences, fear, stress or something else. You will learn how they affect your life from work to school to your relationships and more. Plus how low self-esteem can increase the chances of stress, depression and dependency on alcohol, drugs or bad habits.

Next I will show you how to access your inner voice and to become an observer of your mind. You will learn to challenge the beliefs you have about yourself and reframe them to optimize yourself. Like a surgeon you will discover how to extract any toxic mind-tumours and restore a healthy life balance. Once you start to realize that a negative belief of yours is not a concrete fact you can open the pathway to greater things in your life. All of us have goals and through using this powerful way of building lasting self-esteem you will be better able to rise above and over the challenges. Change your thoughts and you will change your life.

In the next chapters I will show you how to retrain your brain by forming stronger pathways to pave the way for higher self-esteem. Discover the power of the language and how it shapes the world around you. In addition you will discover the inner workings of human motivation and how it will help you to realize your fullest potential.

Moving on I will discuss significant research which has revealed that those who struggle with being vulnerable, lead unhappy lives. Through being vulnerable, accepting yourself and sharing you can start to have a healthier level of self esteem. Sharing and being vulnerable is also the key to emotional intimacy in relationships. All of this can be done without living for the approval of others or without crying into the pillow every night.

In the next chapters body image issues are addressed. Body image is one of the most common reasons that people struggle with their confidence. The media and society portray unrealistic expectations that people feel lost about and fail to live up to. I will show you how this is hurting your self-esteem and confidence. Plus the symptoms to watch out for and how you can work on them. Additionally I will reveal how performance anxiety and sexual dysfunction in the bedroom can be overcome without needing expensive treatment or drugs. All of this will lead to much more positive and fulfilling sexual and romantic experiences for both partners.

In the socializing and charisma chapter I address the ways in which people struggle socially. Maybe you are anxious about going out and meeting new people. Or maybe you want to be more confident in social situations. I will show you some easy ways to be more social, eliminate the fear of rejection and overcome social anxiety. I will also show you how to become charismatic in your own unique way without being a copycat. Additionally many people fall into bad habits of trying to please people and making a good impression at the sake of their integrity and happiness. Understand that your life is in your hands and anything you do should not be at the sake of your happiness and someone else's.

In the last chapter about work and relationships I cover the main reasons that affect people's confidence and self-esteem in the workplace and in their love lifes. If you struggle to get your point across at work or if you always feel like you're not getting anywhere in your career and love life then you will benefit from this. Learn to be assertive and well received. Additionally if you've been single for a while or if you are in a relationship where there is constant arguing, blame and criticism then discover how you can build better relationships.

The conclusion will wrap up everything that has been covered and give closure to the book. Including the one thing I want you the reader to take away from this book. Additionally at the end of each chapter are some exercises that will help you cement the knowledge into your new improved mindset and further increase your self-esteem and confidence. Please take the time to do each exercise in this book and you will gain the most value from them.

Understand that you are not your thoughts and they don't rule who you are. You can change them and make them more empowering. Once you do that your life will start to improve. That might sound easier said than done but when you apply just a little bit of effort to become more positive in your thoughts everyday it starts to compound. Yes it will take some work to create a healthy sense of self-esteem and it begins with taking full responsibility for your life.

"All that we are is the result of what we have thought."
~Buddha

Imagine being able to meet new people effortlessly. Or to get up on stage and deliver a killer presentation. The world becomes a place where you're accepted for who you are. Don't waste years of your life hiding away. No one is going to come and rescue you. The responsibility to change ends with you and that power is in your hands to become the best you can. Now let's begin.

"It ain't how hard you hit… It's how hard you can get hit and keep moving forward." - Sylvestor Stallone

Understanding Self-Esteem and Confidence

In order to skyrocket your self-esteem and confidence it is crucial that we understand them and how they are influenced. Confidence simply puts our feelings about our abilities to perform various actions, tasks and functions. Whilst self-esteem concerns the way we feel about ourselves, how we think, our body image and if we feel worthy or not. It is possible for someone with healthy-self esteem to have low confidence. For example someone might have healthy self-esteem but still lack the confidence to talk to strangers. It is also possible for someone to have low self-esteem but to be confident. For example a rich person who is confident in making money but lacks self love.

Self-esteem and confidence affects;
- How much you like and value yourself
- Your ability to recognize your self worth and assert yourself
- Your ability and openness to trying new or difficult things
- Kindness towards others and yourself
- How you feel about your past
- How you feel when your alone or with others
- Beliefs about whether you matter
- Beliefs about what you deserve

Self-esteem

Self esteem in the simplest of terms defines how you feel about yourself. The feeling is a result of situations and experiences that have shaped how you currently view yourself. When someone has low self-esteem they hold bad inner feelings. Feelings of being awkward, unloved and useless are all too common. The inner critic is particularly strong and they are easily hurt by others. Their default focus tends to be on the negatives, both real and imagined. Low self-esteem hurts people in many ways. It causes them to experience problems at work, school and in relationships. Chances of stress, depression and dependency on alcohol, drugs or bad habits are also increased. Worst of all is that this causes negative reinforcement of low self-esteem and traps people.

People with high self-esteem value themselves more positively. They believe in who they are and value their presence in the world. Positive traits of high self-esteem include being rational, independent, creative and open. Criticisms are accepted by them and they are better able to overcome difficulties. This allows them to maximize their potential and as such to live a better quality of life.

Confidence

Confidence is closely related to self-esteem. Confidence is a state of mind, of accepting who you are and feeling good about yourself. Broadly speaking it's about believing in yourself, your skills and abilities. In essence it is having faith in yourself and determines how effective you believe you can be. Ultimately it forms your courage to try new things, take risks, grow and learn from your mistakes. Having a healthy dose of confidence makes everything positive in your life increase. You will be stronger to take life on, accept new challenges and achieve your goals much easier with confidence.

Confidence is not a static state of mind. None of us are born with high or low confidence. Depending on the situation and your level of experience it fluctuates. For example, you might be confident in sports but have low confidence when it comes to public speaking. But don't worry too much about having confidence in everything because that's impossible. Most important is to have a generally high all around confidence level. The more you work on it, the easier it will become for you to use and maintain.

From an early age we learn from others how to think and behave. Add to that the experiences of life we have had in different situations. All of which affect our confidence. When a person has faced harsh criticism, failure and negative experiences it can result in having low confidence. Maybe you were embarrassed at a public speaking event and it hurt your confidence when you now try public speaking. Or maybe you were picked on at school because of your height and this crushed your confidence.

Low confidence prevents us from doing the things we want because we fear people will laugh at us or we will make a mistake. It stops us from living the life we deserve. On the other hand when a person is too confident it can rub other people up the wrong way. You might be perceived as arrogant or narcissistic. Naturally as you become more confident it can be easy to fall into the trap of thinking you're better than others. There is a fine line between confidence and arrogance. It's important that you understand the differences so that you are received positively in your interactions with people.

Arrogant people usually believe that they know it all and that they have nothing to learn from others. They fight to be right and to show others they are wrong. This makes them bad listeners who default to talking about themselves and are not particularly humble people. They will brag about themselves and seek the spotlight at any given opportunity. On a conscious and unconscious level there is a distinct power play. By them putting others down and themselves up they are attempting to gain advantage over others. Usually this comes from a place of masking some underlying insecurities.

Confident people are much better listeners and team players. They listen to others and shine a light on others achievements. They encourage teamwork and are ready to give praise at any given opportunity. Confidence comes from true self belief, it is pure coming from the heart and not from any comparision or power play. There is no bragging or acting superior to others here.

Clearly arrogance pushes people away. Nobody would want to be around an arrogant person because they don't make them feel good. Conversely confident people are attractive to be around because they inspire others. Time spent around a confident person is usually time well spent since confidence is contagious. Of course sometimes an arrogant person may be more competent and skilful than a confident person, but the confident person will endeavour to act with more integrity and thought for others. Take this in mind.

What are the causes of low self-esteem and confidence?

Self-esteem and confidence changes from day to day and there are certain things that affect them. These differ from person to person. Below we will explore some of the most common causes.

Childhood and life experiences

Low self-esteem issues often begin in childhood. Various life experiences can result in individuals having low level self-esteem. For example if someone was the victim of emotional or physical abuse then it can affect their feelings of self worth. Often they will replay those hurtful memories over again and will be forever tormented by them. For some reason, the message that you are not good enough is a message that stays with you.

Parenting style can also affect self-esteem. If your parents constantly put you down and belittled you then it's likely that you still carry the wounds. Maybe it was your parents own struggles with abuse that they then inflicted onto you. Encouragement of children is really important to their self-esteem. Lack of encouragement will likely cause lower self-esteem.

From birth babies look to their parents for appreciation with every new thing. It is an innate thing. Imagine a child taking part in a competition and getting second place or getting a good grade. Without recognition and encouragement from their parents they might be less likely to give it their full effort the next time. Or worse they might give up. On the other side though too much praise or over protection can hurt a child's development. If this happens then the child will be too dependent on their parents' opinions. It's important to strike a good balance of praise and protection.

Additionally bullying, humiliation and harassment during childhood all can negatively define someone's self-esteem. This could even happen in later life such as the workplace where people might treat you wrong and in turn hurt your self-esteem. Furthermore your gender, sexual orientation and race might also be a cause for people to bully or harass you. If you have been on a victim of discrimination then it might have resulted in some internal negative dialouge about whether you belong.

Whether we had a good or bad childhood or suffered from abuse the fact of the matter is that it is in our past and we need to let go of that. You cannot control what has happened before but you can control what happens now. Right now you're in control of the processes and events in your life. Don't let the past dictate that. It can be easy to blame others for the things that happened in your life. But that will only take you so far.

Genetics & Mental Health

Various studies have concluded that our genetics determine how much confidence boosting chemicals our brain has access to. The main chemicals are serotonin and oxytocin which are associated with happiness. Both of these are inhibited by our genetic variations.

Mental illness is likely to affect an individual's self-esteem. At the receiving end quality of relationships, work and life in general suffer. Upon being diagnosed with a mental illness it's only normal for someone to have a negative emotional reaction. Ultimately that influences their self-esteem. This is natural and you need to allow yourself time to build back. Whilst on the road to recovery your confidence will be going up and down but it will get better. The pursuit towards confidence will be one of hard work but the rewards are going to be worth it.

Age

Age also has a big influence on our confidence. As we age our bodies change and we encounter many life changing events such as retirement, loss of loved ones, health issues and so on. Confidence and self-esteem in a person typically follows a bell curve that slowly rises from the late teen years and starts to peak at middle age. It then starts to decline after the age of around sixty. At midlife people tend to be in their highest positions of power and status. Later in life they have less responsibility, activity, socializing and movement. But it doesn't need to be that way. Of course we can't always do everything we once did. But we can still try new things and stay active. Keep taking pride in your appearance, wake up and get dressed like you were going to work. You're never too old to try new things and live a full life.

Temperament

All of us are unique in our own ways. Dad might be an easy going person but maybe your sister is always tense. Temperament is wired into us from birth and continues into adulthood. A calm baby becomes a calm adult and so on. These personality differences are what define temperament which influence our behaviour and emotional responses.

Now that doesn't mean to say that your temperament stops you from feeling a broad range of human emotions. Everyone has happy or sad days. Overall temperament relates to your general demeanor and reaction to life. Even if you're predisposed to some negative traits it is still possible to peacefully coexist with your temperament. All it takes is a little work. You won't be able to change your innate self but by working with a therapist you will be able to counteract your basic temperament. This will help you to discover how it might be negatively affecting your life. Temperament doesn't have to define you, as long as you're willing to reach out for help.

Fear

Fear is a serious obstacle to confidence and self esteem. When you're in fear it's hard to move forward. Fear paralyzes and focuses a person's mind onto the negative. But it is not a burden that they have to carry forever. Facing your fears is the pathway to becoming your best self and in order to do that you need to identify the drivers behind your fearful thoughts.

What would you say if I asked you to approach an attractive stranger? How about if I asked you to travel to a new country next week? Or try a new extreme sport? One of the biggest fears is the fear of the unknown. When faced with new or challenging situations people often feel less confident. An important factor of dealing with fear is to prepare and plan for the unknown. Perhaps you're going to a networking event. Practice some default answers to standard questions or script out some opening lines. Or maybe you have a driving test coming up. Rehearse in your mind all the areas you will need to be tested on. Hire a teacher and come well prepared.

When you are more prepared it will make you more confident in the situation. With adequate learning and research you can gain a better understanding of unknown situations you might be facing. Ultimately you need to be in control of the unknown situations as much as you can. This will make you more calm, collected and confident. For example, if you're in a recession and you're about to lose your job then study about what to do in a recession. Or for example if you're a first time parent. You will probably have a lot of anxiety about having your first child. Your confidence will be low in this area. But if you both study, go to support groups and ask parents who were in the same situation as you then you can gain more confidence. Then when the baby is born you can apply this knowledge, gain experience and even more confidence. Take the knowledge and put it into practice. When you practice what you learn it will build even more confidence.

When you consistently expose yourself to fear you will build more self-esteem and confidence. Not every attempt will be successful and you might go backwards at times. But if you stay consistent towards facing your fears then it is one of the best ways to build self-esteem and confidence. Confidence in fact comes from overcoming obstacles rather than the common misconception that it is coming from accomplishments.

Stress

Stress can worsen self-esteem and confidence significantly. According to studies by European scientists, women who are suffering from stress during their pregnancy have an increased risk of giving birth to children with diseases.

When the going gets tough keep thinking big. Essentially you will need to be a confident person in order to stay calm and relaxed during the most stressful experiences. Life throws challenges at us all the time. In fact right now the world is going through a pandemic. Borders are closing and people are being confined to their homes. How you deal with this and the aftermath will depend on how you deal with the stress.

During challenging times like this it is important to remain optimistic. Take the focus off of yourself. Avoid the negative news and try spreading something positive or inspiring. Try to lift people's spirits. How much social support a person has can influence the amount of stress they have. In addition a physically stronger body is going to also be an emotionally stronger one. Combine a good social group with regular exercise and your stress will be reduced. All of this will fill up your self-esteem tank and make you a happier and more confident person. Otherwise stress will arise and that will impact your confidence negatively.

Shame

Shame involves feelings of unworthiness around others. This can be a huge problem because it puts a wall between connecting deeply with others. Often people with a history of abuse bear the scars of shame. It drives their behaviours and thoughts. Particularly with men it manifests in trying to prove themselves or hiding away. Sadly a shame is often the result of sexual abuse.

As children grow older they become aware of what others think of them. It can be difficult with shame to accept praise and often they default to shame because fundamentally they feel insecure as a person. This can be made even worse if a parent ignores their child. Or whenever the child makes a mistake the parent puts them down and shames them with insults or physical abuse. Experiencing these things repeatedly leaves them feeling bad, unloved, and shameful. Basic needs for love are met with rejection and abuse. When this happens over years it becomes difficult for them to form intimate relationships. Yet with self awareness and understanding it can be beaten. Many other people have done it and lived to become proud of who they are. Stay tuned on how you can become proud also.

Isolation

According to various surveys many Americans report that they have no one to talk to about important matters. In almost twenty years between 1985 to 2004 this has increased from ten percent to over twenty five percent. Whilst in a 2010 European Social Survey, over twenty five percent of the people surveyed only met with people socially just once a month or even less frequently. Then in the UK between 1996 and 2012, the proportion of people aged forty five to sixty four years old who lived alone has risen to over fifty percent.

Social isolation is particularly common amongst the older generation. But it can be experienced at any stage of life. This is why people who recently become unemployed often experience a loss of confidence. It wasn't the job loss but more so the social isolation that brought about those feelings.

Ultimately social isolation can be devastating, causing increased mortality and health problems.

Reducing the amount of time we isolate ourselves is both important not only for our self-esteem but most importantly for our quality of life. Right now we are experiencing the effects of forced isolation and "social distancing" due to the pandemic. This has highlighted the issues of isolation. But there are still things you can do right now. Calling friends and family is one. Greeting your neighbours is another. Or even taking action by engaging in some online communities. Make yourself feel like you matter in this world.

Avoidance

Avoidance is a powerful defense mechanism. People suffering from avoidance often think of themselves as being flawed and appealing to others. They will be overly apologetic or submissive. Often they view themselves with contempt and rather choose to be alone than risk social rejection or humiliation. Those individuals will relate to being anxious, lonely and unwanted by others.

Often it kicks into gear without your awareness. That can be really trivial everyday situations such as going to the supermarket or even answering the phone. In the worst cases going to work can bring on feelings of anxiety. You spend hours in the mirror getting ready but you're never happy with what you see. Or you don't feel confident and so you call in sick at work. Eventually you find that your discomfort about meeting new people has turned into panic. Just the thought of these situations now fills you with terror. At this point it feels safer for you just to stay home and avoid all social connections.

Some type of avoidance is fine and it can allow us to reflect or release stress. For example spending some time alone to think. Just be aware of whether your avoidance is creative or if it is dysfunctional. To help you determine, ask yourself if the activity is freeing you or if it is binding you? Is it helping you move forward with your life?

Avoidance comes at a cost. Sure it might feel like you're safe in the short term from social anxiety but having people to share life with and confide in is a proven source of long term happiness. There is a whole world out there full of adventure and happy experiences. But the more you avoid the smaller your world becomes and life is wasted. Instead of watching TV at home, go out to the cinema. Instead of listening to music go to a concert. Meet your friends. Life is out there.

Seeking comfort in avoidance only makes things worse. Danger is that the more people fall into unconscious avoidance habits the deeper the habits form. In psychology terms this is known as negative reinforcement. Negative reinforcement refers to any kind of behavior that's rewarded because it removes an unwanted feeling. For example if you suffer from social anxiety. Say it makes you uncomfortable meeting new people. So you begin to avoid any social activity, which makes you more uncomfortable just meeting your friends and leads to more avoidance. This is a form of negative reinforcement because the so-called reward is that you don't have to experience the fear anymore. But why waste years of your life neglecting what you want?

To combat this you need to learn to face the uncomfortable situations without avoiding them. Practice being mindful. Most anxiety and fear is anticipatory which means what you actually fear is what might happen instead of what actually is happening. In fact this fear of an unknown future is often worse than reality. Being mindful brings your attention to the present moment and stops you getting stuck in anticipatory anxiety. Staying focused and in the moment. Change is possible when we discover how to not let fear dictate our actions.

Perfectionism

Perfectionism is a flawed way of thinking that a person must have everything figured out before taking any action. They are never enough and that keeps them from taking action. Companies are constantly advertising their products to make you feel bad about yourself and that you're not enough.

From a young age we are told that beauty and money are the keys to success and confidence. Ideals are portrayed all day, everyday in films, TV, music and media. Rich guy gets a girl. Beautiful person is successful. But this isn't the truth. It is a false reality. Who do you think is happier? The rice farmer in a rural country, surrounded by his loving family who loves his work. Or the rich lonely billionaire who hates his work and is surrounded by people who despise him but deceive him to get close to his money?

Social media and the general media brings inadequacies even more into our awareness. Everyone appears to have the perfect marriage, career and model looks. However we must be aware that the media and in particular social media is carefully curated to show the highlights of someone's life. Everyone has self doubt, bad days and physical flaws but they don't share them on social media.

Social media can be a good thing to keep you connected with friends and family but it's crucial that we stay aware of how we perceive others or measure ourselves to them. In the modern world it's all too easy to constantly be comparing yourself to others. More often than not this happens when you look at social media. Naturally as humans when we look at social media we compare ourselves to others. Either you feel bad about yourself because their life looks better than yours or judge others to make yourself feel better.

Stop comparing yourself to them. Only compare yourself to who you used to be. When you look at other people or celebrities who you consider to be rich, famous, beautiful and successful keep in mind that no one is perfect. Most of or in fact all photos posted online these days have been heavily edited, filtered and perfected. Plus you don't know their back story or struggles. You're just seeing a highlight and reality is not like that.

The truth is that if you value yourself and are grateful for what you have then that's going to give you real lasting self-esteem and confidence. How much money or how beautiful you are has zero reflection on your identity. When we connect our self worth to money and beauty we can easily fall into negative thought patterns. You start comparing yourself to others. All the internal dialogue sends you into fits of anxiety.

Say you are a confident football player who has played since you were a kid. In fact you're really quite good at it. But that doesn't mean you won't make mistakes from time to time or that you're better than all the other players out there. True confidence in this regard means you are sure you can handle pretty much anything on the football pitch.

When it comes to trying things we are not familiar with it comes down to how we handle our mindset and emotions. Those with a growth mindset are sure they can figure it out and are willing to grow. Fixed mindsets struggle with obstacles and overcoming them. The reality is that we will fail at some point but the future lies in how we deal with adversity. Do we stay down? Or do we rise again?

Fail forward towards success and get comfortable with the uncomfortable. Many people avoid these challenging situations because of the pressure they put on themselves. They expect to be perfect. They expect themselves to have perfect conversations, presentations and performances. The reality is that even the best of us aren't going to be perfect one hundred percent. Look at the top performers. There is always room for improvement. Set your expectations realistically. If you fail, understand that you're going to be ok. It's no big deal. The more you practice that detachment from outcome and trying new challenges then the more fear disappears and your self-esteem and confidence will grow.

Negative People

Who you surround yourself will significantly influence the way you feel about yourself. It's often quoted that you are the average sum of the five people that you are spending the most time with. If those are negative people then you need to make changes to your social circle because they will just drain your energy and turn you into a more negative person. The sooner you can identify and move away from negative people in your life the better. Ask yourself after spending time with someone. Do I feel tired or do I feel energized?

Set yourself some boundaries of what you will and will not accept from people. If someone is bad to you and they are not adding value to your life then tell them to fix up or walk away. Additionally if you're currently in an abusive relationship then this will of course cause you to have lower self esteem. The longer you're in it the harder it becomes to leave. It feels like your world is shrinking and your abusive partner is dominating it. Some days they are kind and it makes you forgive them but you're just trapped in a negative cycle and you need to break it. Set some boundaries or make your exit plan. You deserve better.

Bad habits

Low self-esteem issues can lead to a dependency on or excessive consumption of drugs, alcohol sex and other destructive behaviours. Furthermore this can spiral out of control into crime, sex addiction and major life problems. The short term effects of drugs, alcohol and so on may indeed bring pleasure at the start but that is only a temporary effect. Long-term abuse can lead to serious health and life problems.

Alcohol and drugs disrupt the brain's functions which affect feelings, thoughts and in turn actions. Chemical changes weaken inhibitions and create an increase in confidence which is often why people with low self-esteem are attracted to using them. They get a hit of fake confidence but then they become dependent on it. The downside is that it can spill over into poor performance, lead to aggression, anxiety and depression.

Drugs in particular are known to cause mental health issues. Many cases cause psychosis which is directly related to self-harm and suicide. In the UK The National Health Service (NHS) have recoreded that over half of the deaths from suicide were from people who had a history of drugs and alcohol abuse.

Human motivation

Understanding self-esteem helps us to realize who we are and to effectively face our challenges in life. This helps us to move towards our goals, better motivate ourselves and have a clearer life direction. A person with high self-esteem believes in themselves and has the motivation to go after their goals. Motivation is in essence our own individual drive to achieve. When you're motivated to take on tasks and activities towards your goals then it raises your chances of success. As a catalyst it also raises your self-esteem even more because you are becoming more accomplished.

Maslow's Hierarchy of Needs

Abraham Maslow developed a theory on the hierarchy of needs in which he explained that people have growing needs. People are more motivated and have higher self-esteem when their needs are met. Needs begin at the lower order and rise to a higher order. Once lower order needs are met another set of needs will arise until eventually self-actualization is fulfilled. The order of needs are as follows.

Physiological needs

Physiological needs are the basic essentials that a person needs to live. Such as food, water, shelter, air, clothes and so on. When a person is hungry they can only think of food. When you are working, your job pays you money to take care of your needs for basic necessities.

Security / Safety needs

Once physiological needs have been met the need for security and safety arises. This concerns the things such as having a job, being safe from any danger and so on. People aspire to these needs and tend to pursue higher levels of safety and security until those needs are fulfilled.

Love / belonging needs

Humans are naturally social beings. We find that friends and family become an essential part of our life. With the next level of security and safety needs met a person wants to feel that they belong to a particular group. Having a sense of belongingness creates feelings of being wanted and loved in a person.

Self-esteem needs

Once the two previous needs have been met, a person starts to feel higher levels of self-esteem. They feel the need to be respected, appreciated, and to have power in the world. This fills them with confidence and is manifested in examples such as a want for being recognized for achievements.

Self-actualization needs

This is the highest level in the hierarchy and can be thought of as a person's desire to reach a certain level of success. For example, say an employee strives to become a CEO and after many years of diligence they finally achieved it. That would be the peak of their career and the realization of their dreams.

Exercise

Building self-esteem can be achieved through small daily steps. Find something to do everyday that makes you feel good.

Discover the activities that put you into a state of happiness, flow and joy. Depending on what you like to do most, maybe that's going to the gym, reading, meeting friends, cooking or whatever else you enjoy. Or take time out to enjoy the simple pleasures of life, from watching a sunset to playing with your children or enjoying a beer. It should be something that is rewarding.

Commit to doing it everyday for one month.

How Do You Stop Negative Thoughts?

The human mind never stops. Have you ever stopped and taken awareness of what thoughts are going on inside of your mind? We now know that negative thinking creates a variety of psychological problems which can impact the quality of our life. Studies have proven that when groups of people focus on either the positive or negative outcomes of an event that those who focus on the negatives will almost always suffer from low self-esteem. Negative thoughts cloud our vision and create feelings of helplessness.

In order to improve your self-esteem you need to know where you are right now. You need to identify the internal dialogue that plays on repeat in your mind. Sometimes it's healthy but other times it could be negative. When it's negative you think toxic thoughts which cause bad feelings and low self-esteem. When comparing a healthy and confident mind with a weak one you will find that the healthy mind always has a more positive inner dialogue.

Later in this chapter I will show you how to effectively reprogram any negative mental self talk into something more positive that will build your self-esteem. But one thing I want to make clear first is that no matter how positive you are, there will always be negative feelings or thoughts creeping into your mind from time to time. That's normal, no one feels positive one hundred percent of the time. Overall we just need to cultivate a generally more positive mindset with less unnecessary doubt and negative thoughts.

Beliefs

Beliefs are at the core of who you are as a person. The beliefs we have about ourselves are formed from answers to direct and indirect questions we ask of ourselves from our experiences. Understanding how your beliefs influence your life is essential. Belief systems are the foundation of how people view the world around them. The beliefs we hold come from the sum of our past experiences. From the moment we are born we are trying to figure out the world around us. We learn that a car drives us somewhere, that our parents will take care of us, that food fills us up and so on.

Every aspect of your life is influenced by your beliefs. From the level of intelligence you hold to the decisions you make to the questions you ask of yourself. Some beliefs are helpful and others are not so helpful. Maybe they will help you to solve problems, or maybe they will bring bad events to your life or determine the things you will or won't do. If your beliefs are not aligned with your goals then it's going to be difficult to achieve them. Ultimately they might hold you back in your life and relationships.

Challenge your beliefs

Identify the areas where you need to change your thoughts. Maybe you are always negative about your work, love life or social life and so on. Once you have identified the things that cause you to think negatively pay attention to your thoughts here. Ask yourself if these thoughts are really truthful. Would you say them to a friend or out loud in public? Challenge your thinking and test how accurate your thoughts are. Are your views factual? Do they make logical sense? If it helps write them down the answers to those questions. If there is an area of your life which you are not happy about the results with then its likely you have a limiting belief there. Consider the following areas:

- *Finances: Do you have any financial difficulties in your life? Do you have everything you need and want? How much money do you have saved? Is your income what you want it to be?*
- *Relationships: Do your relationships make you happy? This includes your lover, friends, family and coworkers.*
- *Health: Are you feeling good about your body? How is your weight and overall health?*
- *Fun: Are you living the life you want? Is there anything that you dream of doing?*
- *Is there any other aspect of your life in which you're experiencing dissatisfaction?*

Make a list of all of your beliefs, both negative and positive to the challenges you identified above. Be one hundred percent honest with yourself here.

Here's a short example around health:
- *I'll never be healthy.*
- *People like me can't build muscle.*
- *I'll never be fit enough to run a marathon.*
- *Whenever I go to the gym I get tired easily.*

Here's another example around money:
- *I'll never be rich.*
- *I'm not smart enough.*
- *I'll never have enough money.*
- *I always make bad decisions.*

Now can you see why it would be really hard to become healthy or wealthy when you believe things like "I'm not smart enough" or "I get tired easily"? Once you have taken stock of your negative beliefs I want you to put them in order. Start with the belief that is causing you the most difficulty. Then order the rest in a hierarchy of greatest to least negative impact. When you have an ordered list of negative beliefs it's time to take steps to change them. Read them out and ask yourself.

- *Is this really true?*
- *Have I experienced this enough to confirm it is true?*

- *Am I one hundred percent sure?*

Once you start to realize that a negative belief of yours is not a concrete fact you can begin to further explore if there is actually any at all truth in it. Essentially you are weakening the beliefs that limit you. Consider evidence that is contrary to what you believe. For example if you believe that you are a worthless person then consider what your parents or your friends think of you. I'm sure you will find an opposing belief here. Find more reasons and examples why a belief is not real. For example, maybe the people who told you this don't really know you. Or maybe you've never actually experienced this belief in reality. Keep coming up with reasons to weaken your negative beliefs. Search online for people who held similar beliefs and how they overcame or how they are different from you. It doesn't have to be massive facts but the more things you stack up facts against your negative beliefs the weaker they will become. Break the chains that hold you back.

During these stages it's really helpful to keep a journal everyday in which you can write down your feelings. Write down anything positive or negative here. Free flow your mind onto the paper or on your phone. Identify where you need to change and work on yourself. Each day, check in on yourself. Ask yourself about those previous beliefs, do you still feel it? Are you changing? Keep working on your lists of negative beliefs and continue to work on any new negative beliefs that come up. As you grow and set goals new limits will be revealed. Self development is all about that.

Dealing with negative thoughts

Anytime a negative thought comes into your head, observe and assess where it is coming from. Detach, observe it and create distance from you and it. This will help you to realize that who you truly are is separate from any negative thoughts or feelings.

Explore all facets of it and you might learn something. Perhaps it could be presenting an opportunity to explore new solutions to an old issue or problem. Working through negative situations often stimulates growth. As you become more positive it will be easier for you to quickly reframe those negative thoughts into something more positive.

Adjust your thoughts and replace any negative ones that are not true with more accurate and positive thoughts. Trust and encourage yourself. Believe that good things are coming your way. When you face a stressful challenge tell yourself, "I got this". If you screw up, forgive yourself because somewhere along the line everyone makes mistakes. But mistakes don't create your identity; they are just moments in time.

Avoid any 'should' or 'must' statements. Using these words puts unnecessary demands on yourself. You need to set realistic expectations of yourself. Focus on the positives and the things that went well. If you screw up, look at the lessons and find a way to make it work next time. Give yourself more credit when you do win and celebrate your success. Here are some other negative thought patterns you need to be aware of:

- All or nothing thinking.
  You are limited to seeing things as only positive or negative. For example,
    - "If I don't come first place then I suck."

- Mental filtering.
  Your view of the world is distorted because you only focus and dwell on the negatives. For example,
    - "I forget to attach my notes to the email and now my boss will realize I'm a bad employee."

- Turning positives into negatives.
  You discredit any positive achievements of yours. For example,
    - "I only got this job because I was lucky."

- Negative conclusions.
  You default to reaching a negative conclusion even with barely any supporting evidence. For example,
    - *"My wife didn't reply to my text, she must be angry with me."*

- Confusing feelings for facts.
  You mistake your feelings to be factual. For example,
    - *"I feel like a loser, so therefore I must be a failure."*
- Negative self-talk.
  You don't value yourself and constantly put yourself down. For example,
    - *"I am not enough."*

Positive Thinking

Positive thinking is a powerful and proven way of building lasting self-esteem. When you believe you can do something then you will be more likely to persist ahead. Positive mindsets will help you to overcome obstacles, challenges and adversity along the way. Nothing can beat optimism and nothing worthwhile can be done without hope plus confidence.

"Strength does not come from winning. Your struggles develop your strengths." - Arnold Schwarzenegger

Fundamentally, positive thinking is about focusing on your strengths. Most of us spend too much time dwelling on the negatives but if you challenge yourself to focus on a more positive mindset then your chances of success will increase. Make positive thinking your default. Here are a few tips to help you change the way you think about your life and to be more positive about it.

The Good

Write out all the things that you are good at and anything that you need to improve on. Celebrate your strengths and find ways to improve your weaknesses. Write out all the good things you have done in your life. For example, the time you washed mom's car. Or the time you helped that person across the street. Come up with a list of at least one hundred things. From the big to the small.

Gratitude

Cultivate a mindset of gratitude. Be grateful for everything in your life. Every morning and night simply write down or think about three things that you're grateful for. It could be something as small as the pillow under your head. Or something as big as the love of your family. Think about it for a moment. Ask yourself why you are grateful for it and for how that makes you feel. A heart filled with gratitude will struggle to stay negative even in the most challenging of times. It's like kryptonite for negativity. There is always going to be someone worse off than you right now. Be grateful for your life.

Reframe mistakes

We are only humans and all of us make mistakes from time to time. Instead of focusing on the negatives consider how you can reframe them. For example maybe you failed a test. Look at it as a way to become better next time. Or maybe your wife left you, think of it as an opportunity for a new life. Always be turning anything negative into some kind of positive opportunity or relief.

Compliment

Recognize and celebrate when you have done the right thing. The next time someone gives you a compliment, accept it. No questions asked. No returns. Just thanks. Compliment yourself as well. Share it with your family and friends. In addition, compliment people at every opportunity. It can be something simple such as you compliment someone working in the store for doing a good job.

Stay cheerful

In general maintain a cheerful and positive outlook on life. Criticism or complaining is not useful and if you do it, be constructive about it. Don't be a gossip who always complains because it will only dull your experience of life.

Role model

Find someone you know that is very confident. Observe how they behave, move, and interact. Take a note of it. Get to know them more. Try to be around them and ask them about how they deal with different situations. Learning from others through being around them is a great way to let their confidence rub off on you.

Experience

Gaining experience requires courage at first but if you can break it down into small goals it will be much easier to manage. The more experience we have in successfully completing tasks and goals the more our confidence will increase. Take for example dancing. Most people can't dance. They think things such as "I have two left feet" or "I have no rhythm". But then they visit a dance class. During the first classes they stumble around. But the instructor helps them through the steps. They stay calm and quietly persist. In time they get a few steps right and it encourages them to practice more. Soon enough they are a good dancer. Through the experience it is positively reinforcing more confidence to push ahead and become better.

Stay calm

Those who remain calm when the world is losing control are the confident ones. When you have confidence to achieve a task you're probably going to feel more calm when doing it. If you have less confidence then it's likely to make you stressed or nervous. Try to remain calm in stressful situations. Cultivate a calm state of mind and learn to relax. Find a way to channel the stress and anxiety. Try to meditate daily or take deep breaths when you're stressed. Working out is also a great way to cultivate calm.

Self-efficacy

Self-efficacy is the belief in your own abilities to deal with life. It plays a key role in whether or not you actually achieve your goals or not. According to the social cognitive theory developed by psychologist Albert Bandura, a person's attitudes, abilities, and cognitive skills are known as their self-system. Similar to confidence, it is how much a person believes they can succeed in a particular situation. The main difference is that confidence is when someone believes in themself even if they have zero knowledge of an upcoming challenge. Self-efficacy on the other hand is the belief in oneself to achieve an upcoming challenge when they already have some knowledge about what they will be dealing with.

Self-efficacy is one of the most studied parts of psychology and with good reason because it can impact so much of a person from their psychological states to behavior, motivation and much more. All of this determines and influences how we think, act and feel about who we are in the world. From the goals we pursue to our actions, performance and reflections are all dependent on it. ☐To help you understand the concept more take a look at the examples below.

A strong self-efficacy:
- *Challenges are thought of as tasks to master*
- *Focused on the activities they participate in*

- *Strong commitment to their interests and activities*
- *Quick to recover from setbacks*

A weak self-efficacy:
- *Avoids challenges*
- *Lack of belief to achieve challenges*
- *Focuses on negatives and lack of ability*
- *Quickly loses confidence*

Self-efficacy forms in early childhood experiences and continues to evolve throughout life as we learn new skills, have new experiences and understandings of life. According to Bandura, four major sources of self-efficacy exist.

1. Mastery Experiences

Mastery experiences are one of the most effective ways to develop a strong sense of efficacy. When we successfully perform a task it strengthens our sense of self-efficacy. In the event that we fail to adequately deal with a task or challenge it weakens our self-efficacy.

2. Social Modeling

Witnessing other people having success is another important source of self-efficacy. When we see people similar to us in capabilities succeed in their efforts it raises our beliefs that we too can do it.

3. Social Persuasion

People can be persuaded into believing that they have what it takes to succeed. For example, think of a time when someone said words of cheer that helped you to achieve a goal. It could be something simple as someone shouting "one more rep" as you lift weights. Verbal cheer from others helps us to rise above our doubt and focus on doing our best.

4. Psychological Responses

Response to situations plays a critical role in self-efficacy. Our state of emotion, mood and stress levels all impact how we feel about our personal abilities in various situations. For example when a person suffers from being nervous when confronted with public speaking they may develop a weak sense of self-efficacy in those scenarios. People can effectively improve their self-efficacy levels by learning how to manage their stress levels and moods when facing challenges.

Self-efficacy varies from person to person and situation. Some people may have a strong sense of self-efficacy in one area such as work and maybe less in sports. For example people with a strong sense of self-efficacy in their health find it easier to maintain healthy living. Individuals with an overall high level of self-efficacy view difficulties as challenges and persist. When they fail it doesn't mean defeat. They recover and double down on their efforts or look at new ways to overcome them. For those with low levels of self-efficacy challenges are difficult tasks as threats that should be avoided. They tend to give up easily and lack confidence to continue. As a result they are more likely to suffer the feelings of failure and depression.

There are various ways to assess self-efficacy levels in a person. Ask yourself the following questions to help you assess your own self-efficacy levels.

- *Are you able to deal with problems if you work hard?*
- *Do you believe you can succeed in your goals?*
- *Can you easily face challenges when they come up?*
- *When faced with a challenge do you bounce back quickly?*
- *Can you easily stay calm during a challenging time?*
- *When you're under pressure do you perform?*
- *Do you believe that working hard pays off?*

If you answered yes to most of these questions, then you probably have a strong and healthy sense of self-efficacy. But if you answered mostly no then you could use a boost. But don't worry because self-efficacy can be built on and strengthened. In order to do that, consider the sources of Bandura's self-efficacy and how you can integrate them into your life. For example mastery experiences contribute significantly to building self-efficacy. Incidentally Bandura himself identified them as being the most effective path to a stronger sense of self-belief. When you succeed in doing something it gives you faith in your abilities. Set goals that can be achieved but which require a significant challenge. If it takes work and persistence then when you achieve it your self-efficacy will rise.

Secondly Bandura identified that observing others is another important method of building a strong sense of self-efficacy. Study success and how others have put in effort to be successful. But that should not be something easy to do. It will be much more effective if these people faced similar circumstances to you. Maybe they're your friends or countrymen. The more alike you feel you are the more effective.

Seek positive feedback and this will improve your sense of self-efficacy. If you have negative people in your life then avoid them because they will just bring you back. Positive feedback can be small things such as your boss telling you that you did a good job. Or friends complimenting you on your style. When it comes from people you respect it will give you greater confidence in your abilities. Or find people to hit the gym with. With a little extra encouragement you can achieve more.

Finally consider, psychological responses. This requires you to be aware of your thoughts and emotions. If you're always getting stressed out or anxious then it all impacts on your confidence. Find ways to manage your stress and anxiety. Try to replace those beliefs or have stress management techniques such as exercise or more positive self talk. Life is full of challenges but with a high level of self-efficacy you can more effectively deal with them.

Exercise

Become an observer of your mind. Now this might sound somewhat complex. You might think, how does one watch one's own mind? I understand it's a difficult concept to grasp. The way to do this is to take yourself away from your thoughts anytime they happen and look at them as an observer. During this process ask yourself if those thoughts are positive or negative. Take a note of the answers.

- *Thought - thinking about the weather = negative*
- *Thought - thinking about my job = negative*
- *Thought - thinking about the football game = positive*

You don't need to do this every single time you think about something. Of course that would be impossible and unrealistic. What I ask you to do is for the next ten days set an alarm on your phone to go off every hour. At that moment observe what you were just thinking and then note it down in the format above. That's it.

Some of your thoughts might be the same. That's fine, just note them down. Recording this information will make you aware of your negative thoughts. Then you can use the belief reframing exercise outlined in this chapter to challenge and reframe them to be more positive thoughts.

Retrain Your Brain To Reverse Negative Thinking

During the learning process the human brain forms new neural pathways. When starting to learn something new the connection is weak. Stronger pathways are formed through learning and these eventually become habitual. For example when first learning to ride a bike you need to focus on balance, controlling the bike and keeping your eyes on the path ahead. All of this requires plenty of thinking. But the more you practice it the stronger the neural pathways in your brain become and eventually you can ride a bike without thinking.

The human brain works much the same way when it comes to how you think about yourself. From childhood, thoughts are formed and repeated based on the messages and beliefs you have been fed during your life. Perhaps people made fun of you and it caused you to repeat thoughts of never being enough. Or perhaps your parents neglected you and it caused abundant issues. Neural connections in your brain were formed and habitual ways of thinking were created.

Studies have revealed that our internal locus of control which is the source of self-esteem in the brain is related to how well regions of the brain connect. This means that people with stronger connections in this area are more likely to have higher long-term self-esteem. The good news is that this can be strengthened. Just like riding a bike, the more you practice, the stronger the connections will become.

Language

Language is powerful. The words we use both out loud and internally shape our world. Words have the power to transform our emotions and to express our life experiences. They can either inspire us or limit us. Words that are negative, create a negative life experience and this can manifest into psychological problems. Or by simply changing words in your vocabulary it can change how you feel and behave to be more positive.

The average person's vocabulary consists of around two thousand words which is less than one percent of the entire English vocabulary. Of those two thousand we most often use approximately, two hundred to three hundred words. These words form our habitual vocabulary which we frequently use to describe our emotions and life events. But there are so many words out there that we could use to express our ideas and feelings. Turning those into something more positive will cause massive positive change in your external world.

Have you ever thought about the words you use the most? The root of the problem is that our default words are not usually optimal. Take some time to write down all the emotions you usually feel. You might notice that most of these are negative. Write down the top things that bring you negative emotions. For example;

- *When you get stuck in traffic = I'm mad as hell*
- *When you think about money = I'm broke*
- *When you think about relationships = I'm not good enough*

Notice how these can affect your emotions and life experience. What if you listed more positive emotions? How much better could your life be? Words like "broke" are pretty extreme don't you think? Try consciously changing those words the next time they come up. Take out a thesaurus and find other creative ways to express those emotions. For example;

- *I'm mad as hell = I'm miffed*
- *I'm broke = This is temporary and I'm moving towards being a winner.*
- *I'm not good enough = I'm perfectly unique*

Doesn't that sound better? Keep going, this isn't about lying to yourself instead it's about loving yourself better and not killing your confidence. Negative talk and rumination is all a part of human suffering. We all tell our own story with particular words and the words you speak become your world. Make it a priority to use better words.

Metaphor

Metaphors can be used to explain complicated concepts by using something similar to simplify them. For example when explaining how viruses spread quickly instead of going into scientific terminology, you might say something such as, "it's like water spilling out of a plastic bag full of tiny holes".

Many of us use metaphors to explain our psychological states. In cases where people have low self esteem they tend to exaggerate things. For example they might say something like, "it's as if the whole world is against me" or "everyone hates me." Fundamentally they have blown things totally out of proportion which of course makes them feel much worse.

Change your metaphors and improve your life. When you stop going to war against yourself then life becomes a whole lot easier. Much like the words you use, for the metaphors you use you need to find more empowering alternatives. For example:

"It's like the whole world is against me" = "A bad day doesn't make a bad life, tomorrow things will be better"

"Everyone hates me" = "Well, you can' please everyone"

The difficulty here is that most people resist changing. Even if they want to sincerely change they still struggle and persist in problematic behaviours. For example, just think of people who are addicted to smoking, yet they still keep cigarettes in the house. Or for example, think of someone who has anxiety issues but he never leaves the house. Metaphorically speaking they are "digging themselves into a hole". The ladder out of that hole is to practice self-observation of the metaphors and language you use.

Take at least thirty minutes out of your day everyday to do nothing except be free to think. Observe and note what comes up. Are there any repetitive negative emotions? Or maybe there is something that bothers you from the past. How would you describe it? What words or metaphors would you use? Through regular practice of self-observation you will gradually become detached from negative self-talk.

Cognitive behavioral therapy

Cognitive Behavioral Therapy (CBT) is a novel treatment of psychological problems and low self-esteem. Professional therapy in the case of CBT can be a big step to take. If that seems too big a step then local support groups can help. These groups will allow you to meet others in an informal setting and talk about how you feel about yourself. This can do wonders for your self-esteem.

People with low self-esteem generally have a low confidence based on assumptions that in some way they are not good enough. CBT helps them to consider more helpful, realistic ways of thinking about their abilities. Instead of focusing on early developmental issues, relationships and history it targets problems in the present moment. Flawed negative thinking is identified and replaced with more useful thinking patterns. CBT proposes that these beliefs are not facts, they are merely opinions that are maintained by unhelpful thinking and behaviours.

CBT involves identifying patterns of thinking and errors in your mindset that are not helping you. Then it retrains your brain to think in a more balanced way that makes use of more functional behaviours. It utilizes various strategies to challenge your limiting beliefs and see if they stand up to factual evidence. Then when it's proven that they do not it then aims to identify alternative 'rational' thinking about the way things really are and develop more helpful behaviours.

For example when someone is ignored by another person they might suddenly assume that it's because they are not good enough. But a more balanced way of thinking is that maybe this other person was just busy and forgot to reply or maybe they didn't even see your message. They had their own problems to deal with. Instead, with this more balanced way of thinking you wouldn't just give up on yourself and sulk. No you might actually call this person and see if they're alright. You would be on a higher level of consciousness and thinking more rationally about the other person's point of view.

CBT also includes some of the following important methods.

- Systematic exposure

Are the situations you fear as bad as you think? In most cases probably not but that enhanced fear often prevents people from taking action. Systematic exposure practices exposing people to situations that they would normally try to avoid. Evidently the results often prove that it's not so bad after all. As a result their anxieties and fears diminish. Practicing systematic exposure will gradually raise your confidence and in order to practice it you will need to make plans to do activities you are not so confident about. For example, that could be things such as attending speaking classes, or going out on dates and so on.

- Mindfulness training

Mindfulness is all about being in the present moment. Right now take awareness for how you're feeling, the air around you, what you hear, see and feel. It is a skill that helps people stop getting caught up in thoughts and worries. It stops people being too critical and in turn improves confidence. Mindfulness can be cultivated through daily practice of meditation. That doesn't necessarily mean going to a monastery. Meditation can simply be taking ten minutes out of a day to sit there and be in the present moment. Detach from your thoughts and focus on the now. You can even do this by simply taking a walk. The more you practice it the stronger your mindset and confidence will become. If your interested to learn more, I suggest checking out work on this by Eckhart Tolle and the waking up app by Sam Harris.

- Problem solving

Problem-solving therapy encourages people with low self-esteem to take a more active approach towards solving their problems. Real and imagined. Instead of being a victim and passively allowing things to happen to them it helps them to seek what they truly want and to go for it. The practice involves setting targets you want to happen and boundaries against what you will not accept. As a result of going after goals the effects on your self-esteem will positively compound.

Goals

Goals play an important role in human motivation and building confidence. Goals are challenging, they will test you, stress you out and at times even make you doubt yourself. But in the path towards greatness you must learn to overcome the challenges. Sometimes you will fail but with confidence you will rise again. The question is how can you set goals that not only build confidence but also lead to fulfillment? The answer is to set goals based on purpose.

One of the worst outcomes for a goal is that you set it and work hard at it. But when you achieve it you feel nothing. This is the result of goal setting without purpose. Often this is the case of trying to gain approval from others instead of for your own gratification. Essentially the goals are not part of your purpose or vision. Instead goals need to be carefully set. Have intent behind them and make sure they will take you somewhere you want to be. They should also develop your skills, knowledge and provide you enough motivation. Ultimately it's about the journey and in this approach goals will be much more satisfying.

The first step is to take complete responsibility for who you are and where you're at right now. Maybe it's time you finally got in good shape or work on building your confidence. Or maybe you have been single for a while and you want to find yourself a great relationship. Take some time out to write out what your skills and potentials are. With clear awareness of your positive attributes and strengths, building self confidence becomes easier. You also need to be aware of your weaknesses so that you can improve on them and later on turn them into strengths. In addition you need to know your values so that your goals are not conflicting with them. Values guide our life and decisions. When we second guess ourselves it's usually because of a value conflict. When you're living according to your values you are going to be on the right path and naturally that will build more confidence.

Make sure that you are setting SMART goals which means they are specific, mesauranle, actionable, realistic and time based. Once you are clear on the goal, break down the goal into small measurable steps. Break them down into yearly, monthly, weekly and daily action plans. Write it out and keep it saved. Schedule each step into your planner or calendar. Saying your going to something is not enough. You need to hold yourself accountable and scheduling it will make this more likely to happen. Give yourself credit when you take action and reward the behaviour. Maybe that's a dinner out or a nice trip somewhere. When you achieve a goal, set a new higher standard.

Personal development and goal setting are similar to physical exercise. In order for it to be effective you need to work on them with persistence and consistency. Everyday you need to take action. Sometimes they might be small actions but they will all add up. That kind of positive momentum will result in massive changes long term.

With enough confidence anything is possible if you're willing to try. Success after all is a matter of averages and possibilities so therefore the more things you try the higher your chances for success are. When you set goals it puts the wheels in motion and pushes you to try more things, to engage in more actions, explore and ultimately get closer to success. The only thing that hinders progress is your level of confidence. When you believe in yourself you are more capable of confronting and jumping over any obstacles.

Remain positive and you will achieve your goals much easier. When the going gets tough stay optimistic, vulnerable and open to new ways. When you have a strong belief in your own abilities it will spill into every area of your life. Don't let confidence fade away, keep working on building it. Set new goals and small steps to take. Celebrate the victories and let them manifest in your confidence.

Push beyond your limits. If you ran 5km last week, run 6km this week. Improve on your results and it will give you more confidence. In order to do this you need to be able to consistently motivate yourself. Find what triggers you to take action. Maybe it's watching others or looking at your past victories. It could even be a healthy dose of frustration to beat your past self. Only compare yourself to who you used to be and no one else. When you do something give it your effort one hundred percent.

Mental shifts will help you to achieve your goals and build confidence. Your mindset is something you have control over. When you're faced with a big goal inevitably will have some negative internal dialogue telling you it's not possible or making up some excuses but despite this voice you can shift your mindset. This will naturally increase your confidence and give you more strength and resilience to push forward. Below are five mindset shifts that will give you more confidence and help you to achieve your goals.

Embrace failure

Failure is a fact of life and it sometimes happens. Don't try to avoid it because otherwise you will just jump from one thing to the next and never get anywhere. Accept that failure will happen. Allow yourself to try new things and learn from the experience.

Accept imperfection

Perfectionists always have an excuse for not trying. It's not the right time or they are not ready yet. They are waiting for the perfect time to take action, but there never is a right time because perfect conditions never exist. Instead jump into opportunities. Now that doesn't mean being careless. It means taking calculated risks. Choose what you want to do, don't try to make it perfect, accept good enough conditions for action.

Let go of control

Life is chaotic and ever changing. No one can control the external world or what others think. Trying to do that will only bring unhappiness and make you feel even more out of control. Let go of all of that stuff and focus on yourself because the only thing you can control is how you respond to life. Ultimately that is what will make you feel in control of your life.

Be comfortable with the unknown

So much fear exists around the unknown and it's a big reason why people accept less than what they deserve. After all it's easier to be comfortable with what you know. Better the devil you know, it could be worse right? But that mentality is flawed because there is no proof that what's out there is worse. In fact it is often better but you just have to be willing to try. If your life sucks then find the courage to take action and discover a better life.

Be curious

A curious attitude to life prepares you for the unexpected and increases the likelihood of you taking action and being creative to solutions. Become curious about life and become a problem solver. Focus on solutions and creativity because it will increase your chances of success.

Purpose

Regardless of age, gender or status everyone deserves a sense of purpose. Human nature desires a feeling or purpose and belonging. Mental and physical health are much higher with a stronger purpose because those people really feel like they have much more to offer. A person with high levels of confidence has a strong sense of purpose.

Exercise

Create a new document on your phone or on a small written journal. For the next ten days identify any negative thoughts or feelings that come up. In addition, write the sources of those feelings. Be honest and it will give you more value. At the end of the day challenge them. Why do I react or feel this way? Then decide on a more positive reaction. For example:

Thought	Cause	Why do I react or feel this way?	Alternative positive reaction
He is a loser	Thinking of colleague	Jealousy, unresolved conflict	Choose not to think of him. Or forgive them.
I'm fat	Looking in the mirror	Overweight. Too much expectation.	Make a plan. Stop comparing yourself.

The Surprising Truth About Being A Man

Men are taught from childhood that real men don't cry. Early on many had to prove themselves and went to great lengths to do so. Aggressive sports, sexual conquests, picking fights, drinking, drugs, outlandish behaviour and so on. Later in life this often manifests into destructive habits such as overspending on lifestyles in an attempt to prove themselves. Victims of trying to prove their manhood, they never feel as if they are good enough.

Modern men are priding themselves on their devotion to work, strength, excelling in sports and accomplishments for which they measure themselves against other men. But those men who adhere to traditional masucline norms such as taking risks, dominating others and trying to control others often experience psychological problems of inferiority, depression and low self-esteem. Significant research has revealed that men who are attached to being perceived as masculine are much more likely to be unhappy.

Men in general avoid talking about how they feel because society has frowned upon that. Guys are taught that "real men" don't show their emotions. Truth is that it's normal to experience emotions such as sadness, depression and shame. Stereotypical masculine men aren't actually strong because inside they fear true expression and acceptance. When we address any issues of insecurity which are completely normal then we can start to overcome them and move towards having a healthier level of self-esteem.

Failure to be authentic and true to your emotions limits the depth of relationships.
Women often complain that they are left confused as to what men are really thinking. Each partner needs to know they are loved and valued. Instead of hiding it needs to be shared. This is a key to emotional intimacy in relationships, which will

improve the connection and depth in all areas of the relationship.

Men and women differ significantly in their sources of emotions and how they express them. What they feel is usually fundamentally different about situations. Men often express their emotions through actions. For example they get angry and it pushes them to take action. Or when they are sad, it makes them want to be alone. If you study the actions of a man you can get a good sense of his emotional state since. Often they would rather express their love for someone through actions rather than saying it. For example they might buy their wife flowers. Or simple coming home from work early instead of going out with friends is an action of love.

The reality is that most men have difficulty with emotions. In particular, talking about and sharing their feelings is not considered a good idea due to socialization and toxic masculinity. Just take a look at father and son relationships. Many fathers are role-models for their sons. Most fathers come from a different era to ours that expects their sons to be more stoic and less emotional. This deep-seated attitude causes problems with the challenges of intimacy. Many men simply shut down and withdraw as a result of facing emotions.

Accept yourself as a man. Express your emotions and vulnerability. It's part of being alive and its part of being a strong person. In order to make progress a man must become aware of his feelings and in doing so he needs to work against years or even decades of conditioning to hide his feelings. Becoming comfortable in expressing vulnerable emotions makes you more empowered and more emotionally healthy. In turn you can become stronger in the face of your pain and more in control of how you feel.

When things go wrong we feel ashamed to talk about it. Maybe you had problems at work or with your partner. But many men seek perfection and struggle to admit their mistakes. Admitting it means we are weak and we would hate that. It could even lead to us losing some perceived status.

Life happens and sometimes bad things happen. Maybe it's some embarrassing mistake. Or maybe something that wasn't even your fault. It's important to remember that it can happen to all of us. Confide in people you trust and love. Friends and family are there for you. You should not feel like a burden. When you acknowledge these feelings it will make you a stronger person.

Think about it another way. Say for example your best friend was struggling and going through a rough time. He needs your support and advice. Would you just let him suffer in silence? Or would you be there for him to confide in you? You already know the answer. The same way of thinking needs to be reflected back on yourself. <u>You need to be your own best friend</u>. Thankfully it's never too late for someone to deal with their vulnerable emotions. With some help any man can become aware of his feelings and master them through friendships and intimacy. That doesn't mean you need to go and cry into the pillow or see a therapist. No, it simply means that you go into your vulnerable feelings, become aware of them and stop blocking them out.

"What is most personal is most universal." - Carl R. Rogers

Masculine Vulnerability

That a strong man must not show weakness is a common misunderstanding. Becoming a stronger man requires one to be honest and vulnerable. Trust is built this way. Now that doesn't mean you have to disclose every single thing about yourself. It's more about sharing the right things with the right people at the right time.

Being vulnerable is a simple and powerful concept. Contrary to popular belief it's not about being all emotional and dramatic or crying. Essentially it is about making a conscious decision to not hide your emotions, feelings or desires. Freedom arises and allows you to express your thoughts, feelings and opinions without worrying about what others think. For example it could be giving someone a sincere compliment without expecting anything in return. Or it could be telling someone how you feel about them sincerely. Situations like these are likely to put you in a position of being rejected and that requires strength because it means you can handle the rejection. You are independent of any outcome. As a great example, there is a scene in the James Bond film Casino Royale where James looks deep into the eyes of his lover Vesper Lynd and says.

"Whatever is left of me. Whatever I am, I am yours."

James bares his soul to her and he isn't afraid to express it. That is being vulnerable. Very powerful and very real. Vesper knows this comes from a place of strength and authenticity. He isn't trying to please her. He is being real with her. There is pure conviction in the statement and he fears no rejection because he is speaking from his heart. Incidentally this is highly attractive and it opens the door to true love.

On a personal side note, I have experienced this before when I first told my girlfriend I loved her. Tears filled my eyes because the emotion was real. At first I tried to hide it but that would have been weak. I told my girlfriend I loved her because it was authentic and I felt it. In the end I exposed my true feelings and I didn't try to hide them. I looked into her eyes as the tears fell down my cheeks. She felt the same and told me so. This was magnificent and memorable for us both.

Another famous example of being vulnerable can be seen in the classic film, Gone with the wind. The lead character Rhett Butler says his last words to Scarlett O'Hara in response to her tearful question as he leaves the home.

"Where shall I go? What shall I do?"
"Frankly, my dear, I don't give a damn"

Rhett shows Scarlett that he has had enough and is ending their failed relationship. He is being vulnerable and one hundred percent authentic. He no longer cares about the outcome.

To check if you struggle with being vulnerable ask yourself the following questions.

- Do you by default move deep conversations to more general subjects because they feel safer?
- Are you working in a job or living in a situation that you don't really like because others caused you to?
- Do you avoid exercise at the risk of feeling shame?
- Does dressing up and going out to socialize make you feel uncomfortable?
- Does the thought of talking to strangers feel awkward?
- Does the thought of asking someone you're attracted to out on a date make you feel uncomfortable?

All of the above symptoms stem from vulnerability issues. From childhood we are taught not to express our emotions. That teaching might have come from learned habits to being disciplined into it. If you struggle with something, hold your hands up and ask for help. Many of us think that we can do it all alone. Truth is that we are hiding our weakness and putting on a brave face. But we can't do everything. There is always someone out there who can do it better. Humble yourself and ask for help. It will get you there much quicker.

That's being vulnerable and that's how you progress. How do you think people achieve success in life? They all have to start somewhere. They all have to reach failure, setbacks and by being vulnerable it invites others to help them. It invites ways to analyze their weaknesses and find ways to improve them. Without this they are hiding in arrogance and covering up their flaws to save face. Foolish and detrimental behaviour. Take for example sports stars. They will often have so many staff and trainers helping them on any given day. They will not hide their weaknesses because they need to work on them to become great athletes. Take full responsibility. Don't be any of the following examples.

- The student who blames his "bad parents" for his poor school performance - Instead if he acknowledged that he was lazy and that he needed to do the work then he would be doing much better.
- The football player who always blames his team for their poor performance or the referee - Instead he needs to look at how he fits into the team and how his blame is affecting the results.
- The guy who complains that all women want is a rich and handsome guy - Instead of looking himself in the mirror and taking account of where he is at and how he can become a better man.

Anytime you blame other people for your life you're handing them control. By doing that it takes the power to change out of your hands. Not only that but you can't control what others think. Sure sometimes you might actually be a victim of a bad situation but you can still step up and make moves to improve it. When you acknowledge a problem and deal with it then that's being vulnerable and it's powerful. Too many of us play it safe and are afraid of being wrong. But face it, all of us make mistakes from time to time. Be able to laugh at yourself and not always take life seriously. If we stay open and are willing to give something a go without fearing failure then we are more likely to progress.

Now some people take being vulnerable too far. They express too much emotion and personal history to others. In effect it comes off as showing yourself as a needy person. It's inappropriate and very off putting. The problem is when people do this they expect it to fix their issues. Instead you need to use it as a way to highlight your issues and take responsibility to address that imbalance. Don't unload it onto others unless they are a trained therapist. Facing it will help you to come to terms with your issues and achieve a healthier emotional base. Become completely accountable for your thoughts, feelings and work on then.

When you are strong enough to expose your weakness and be comfortable with any outcomes then it's very powerful. But by blocking out the opportunity to be vulnerable it is limiting us from truly connecting with others. True connection will result in better relationships and that's what being vulnerable is about. Vulnerability represents a form of deep inner power. With this powerful mindset it attracts the right people into your life and cuts out the ones who are holding you back.

Being vulnerable will offend some people but it is a pathway to living a more authentic life. We all have our flaws and uniqueness, some people will accept those and some won't. For your sake it's better to never hide them and instead find people who you are really compatible with. This will cut out the people from your life who are not important. Just like Rhett and James did. Show yourself, be vulnerable and stop trying to be a perfect person. It will feel tough at times but the more you practice the stronger you become. Put in the work.

Authenticity

Now remember that when being vulnerable you should also do so with authenticity. That's true vulnerability. It's not a trick to get people to like you. Never use it that way. Unfortunately people might tell others what they want to hear for that very reason. If you tell people about your emotional scars such as your personal or family history in a way to get them to like you more than that is just being manipulative.

Authentic vulnerability does not concern what you do, it's more about why you do it. Is the intention behind your behaviour authentic? For example, do you make jokes because you think it's funny or to gain validation? Or would you start a business out of a passion or to try to prove a point to others? Can you see the difference? One is manipulation to gain validation whilst the other is being authentic since it comes from your true intention.

All of us have been told at some point to "just be yourself." But what does that truly mean? Merriam-Webster dictionary defines "authentic" as a quality of being genuine and worthy of belief. Irrespective of the consequences being authentic requires you to be genuine about sharing yourself. More often than not our actions are intended to gain approval or to avoid certain consequences. This can bring troubles to challenging our authenticity and ultimately diminish our self-esteem. Naturally our thoughts become tangled up in excuses as to why we can't do something. This is inauthentic because our words and actions are different from their original intent. We are hiding our true self behind a mask. Little white lies can become consistent and might not seem like such a big deal. But the problem is that the more we change our thoughts and feelings to stay safe in communication the more it limits or self development. We are in effect suppressing our authenticity.

Devolution from our authentic self starts in childhood as we are presented with challenges to our identity. We attempt to cope with challenges by defending against it with inauthentic words and behaviour. Relationships fail to progress because the truth is stuck. In fact a lack of authentic communication is one of the largest impediments to successful relationships. A troubled relationship is often a manifestation of individual challenges projected onto the external relationship. Learning how to communicate with authenticy opens the pathway to a better relationship.

Maybe you feel like you have to act a certain way around your boss. Or you feel there are some things you can't talk about with certain people. So instead you try to fit on or to impress others. We've all felt this way one time or another. But this way is tiring, depressing and it holds us back. To live the life we want we need to give ourselves permission to be ourselves and free from others expectations. It's about living according to your own values and goals. You're responsible, honest and willing to accept the consequences of your authentic intentions.

Yes at times you will have to go against the majority and it might hurt you. This is something you have to accept because in the long run it will make you happier and open you to more fulfillment and opportunity. When you are living an authentic life you don't need to question yourself all the time about whether you said or did the right thing because you have trust in yourself. With that level of trust in yourself you're more likely to trust others and make better judgments of character. People will also respect you for staying true to who you are. Problems are quickly and effectively dealt with. In turn all of this leads to higher levels of confidence, self-esteem and life satisfaction. Being authentic is not something that happens overnight, it's a lifelong journey and requires constant practice. Consider the following.

Values

Authentic living requires you to live according to your values and beliefs. Identify your values. Write them out and commit to living with them. Try what Benjamin Franklin did. Every week score yourself on your values and then let it become a part of your thinking. When you set goals and take actions be sure they align with your values.

Contrast

Who do you want to be? What kind of person are you now? Asking these questions will make it clear about what the contrast between who you are now to who you want to be. Maybe you're not behaving the way you want in your work life. Maybe you're being too passive but you want to be more assertive. Do you see the difference/the contrast? Try to identify these contrasts and work on closing the differences. This is the pathway to becoming more authentic.

Integrity

Preserving your integrity requires courage. Take an inventory of the decisions you make for one week. Your intuition will tell you what is right and wrong. Listen to that intuition and feed it. The more right choices you make the stronger your integrity becomes. Study your choices and ask yourself if they were right. If you make a mistake then own up to it.

Be honest

People tend to avoid being honest because they fear hurting other people's feelings. However honesty requires respecting another person's feelings. Sure in the short term it can hurt them but long term they will come to realize it is the right thing to do. This also means no playing games. Be honest about your intentions and avoid entering into any miscommunication, lying or game playing. Ultimately it will leave a lot of mental baggage behind and bring you to a higher level of consciousness.

No judgment

Humans have a natural tendency to categorize and make assumptions about others. Let go of those preconceived notions and be an empty book. It's easy to fall into this trap. For example a woman wears a short dress and you judge her. Or a man has face tattoos and you judge him. But you should let their actions and behaviour speak first before judging them. Face the world with an open mind and it will return the favour to you.

Learning to accept yourself

A common misbelief in self improvement is the idea that you're a broken person or that you have something wrong with you. Of course everyone has their flaws. The problem is we are living in a world that constantly makes us feel like we are not enough. Marketers and advertisers play on those insecurities of ours. Whilst social media portrays an ideal that is difficult to live upto. The voices are overwhelming and the judgement is strong.

"You're too old for this". "You're too fat". "You're too ugly".

The list goes on and on. But when you accept who you are, the power is taken away from those words and opinions. Self-acceptance means that you're well aware of your flaws but when you recognize them it doesn't hurt your identity. Instead when people condemn you or try to make you feel inferior it goes straight through because you know who you are. Loving yourself defies abuse.

When it comes to self improvement most people and in particular men assume that there is an endpoint to all of it. Self-acceptance is a process that has no end-point. Instead it's a pursuit. In this pursuit you see your flaws, accept and work on them. Life is a journey. Cliche but true. The more you learn, the more you realize that there is much more to learn.

Bruce Lee - "Learning is never cumulative, it is a movement of knowing which has no beginning and no end."

Self-acceptance can help reduce anxiety, shame, shyness and other self-defeating emotions associated with low self esteem. It can also contribute to healthier relationships and better life experience. To truly be able to love someone you must first love yourself. We must recognize that we are responsible for creating our feelings. Yes our history does play a role but for the most it is our thinking about external events that creates our feelings. Regardless of what you thought about yourself in the past you are a worthwhile and unique human. Defeating these self-defeating beliefs and habits requires faith and hard work.

Now it's important to note here that it doesn't mean you accept yourself in neglect of some obvious flaws that can be fixed. Let's be honest if you're overweight or lacking social skills for example then first you need to accept that and work on it. Essentially you need some sort of base standard. For example when you eat food from a restaurant, you expect not to get food poisoning. Or when you're in a relationship you expect not to be abused. In the same regard not being overweight, or something that you can directly control should be set as a base standard by you of what you expect of yourself. Just don't get caught up in what society deems to be a perfectionism. Sales and marketing are built around making people insecure and pursuing solutions through their products. Recognize what your goals are and that they are not the goals of others. Combine self awareness with self acceptance. Make your happiness dependent only on yourself and not what someone else expects of you.

One thing that might come up for you and many others is that they might not want to change or improve. Why not be happy and take what comes? True and with self acceptance you will come to realize that some things are fine just the way they are. Personal priorities are different for all of us and all points of view can be valid on an individual level. Some might decide that setting goals isn't worth the cost of achievement and that they are content with what life brings. Self-acceptance allows you to decide what matters to you. Society will tell you what you need to look like and the way you need to live. But your time and energy should be decided by you.

Exercise

Take responsibility for being a more authentic person based on the following.

Values

Write out your values and score yourself on them each week.

Contrast

Write out answers for who you want to be compared to who you are now. Identify any big contrasts and work on closing the differences.

Integrity

Take an inventory of major decisions you make for one week. Study your choices and ask yourself if they were right decisions.

Be honest

Be honest about your intentions and avoid entering into any miscommunication, lying or game playing.

No judgment

Remove judgment and face the world with an open mind.

The Male Body Image Crisis

Do you suffer from constant negative self-talk about your body? Are you obsessed with your muscle size and shape? Do you avoid events, activities or sports due to body shame?

Body image issues affect millions of men worldwide. An American study of over one hundred thousand men in 2016 highlighted that less than half of the surveyed men were not satisfied with their bodies. Whilst in the UK recent reports highlighted that almost fifty percent of the men surveyed were too self conscious to be seen exercising. In addition many reported that their biggest fears were being seen naked by the other sex.

Negative body image can overwhelm your thinking. It can consume you and diminish your ability to enjoy daily life. Simple things like getting dressed or playing sports bring up all the negative issues. People with poor self image usually believe they look much worse than they actually do. Imagine a person looks in the mirror and they only notice the bad parts of themself. They see things that others don't and believe they possess some defects. It makes them anxious and avoidant of social situations. It can even contribute to the way they carry themselves such as having bad posture which then makes things worse. The way you physically carry yourself affects how you feel mentally. If you're all hunched up or slumped over then your brain interprets it as being stressful and that impacts your emotional state.

Traditionally body image issues have been more thought of as concern to women but they in fact affect people of all ages and genders. Poor body image often causes issues such as excessive dieting, extreme exercising and in more severe cases eating disorders and mental health issues. Many men with body dissatisfaction are hyper focussed on weight loss and muscle building. The negative side effects of this can be over-exercising drugs. Young men such as athletes, bodybuilders and models are particularly vulnerable to feeling insecure about their bodies. This is because they are likely to be judged on their appearance.

Now it is completely normal to feel a bit self-conscious about your appearance and it's normal that there are some things which you might want to change. However when it starts to dominate and occupy the majority of your thinking then its a sign that you need to do something about it. With education, therapy and guidance. Particularly the steps and awareness outlined in this book you can learn to have a healthy body and accept who you are. A negative body image can be a risk factor for many more self-destructive behaviours, including.

- Fad dieting - bodybuilders, athletes, models and young men are often dieting. Many of the diets they use are not always nutritionally sound. For example there is not enough food or there is too much food.
- Food disorders and forced vomiting
- Exercise addiction - many men try to hide their dissatisfaction in over exercise. It ends up taking all of their time and energy.
- Steroid abuse - male groups who are training to develop more muscle are most at risk of using performance and image enhancing drugs. These have numerous negative side effects that can destroy long term health.
- Dramatic weight changes from being overweight or malnourished
- Excessive use of diet pills and laxatives.

Superheroes

Both men and women struggle with their body image concerns but for men they are spoken about much less. Men feel as though they don't compare up to the traditionally masculine body with big arms, small waist. So they suffer in silence and the issue worsens. Genetically many men can never attain these physiques. Not only that but most pictures of ripped muscular men online are heavily curated and edited. Then in the bedroom men place unrealistic demands on their performance. They compare themselves to the toxic mascuilnity spread in porngraphy and locker room small talk.

From an early age men are exposed to an idealized masculine body. Boys play with superheroes and action figures. Subconsciously this is presenting an unrealistic standard to live up to. Men are comparing themselves to ripped and muscular guys as being the epitome of masculinity. Movie stars are effortlessly packing on the muscle to transform into superheroes. This is the new norm. However these kinds of bodies are only attainable to a few. Actors are known for hiring teams of nutritionists and personal trainers. Whilst many Instagram models or muscle men hide the efforts, genetics and the methods required. They make it look like they were born that way. Then there is also the heavy editing of photos. Editors will put so many filters on the images and remove blemishes. Plus they will even make muscles much bigger and more ripped. Tennis star Andy Roddick famously called out a magazine for editing his picture to have bigger biceps and flawless skin.

Today's culture of ideals is full of pressure which is further compounded by social media. Mens magazines in particular are guilty of featuring a ripped adonis on the front cover and promising that every guy can look just like this. Plus all of us have our own genetics and that means for some of us those levels are just not possible.Fact is most of the pictures are heavily curated and they go to extreme lengths for that shot. From extremities such as cutting out water for a day to sucking in their abs and many other tricks. For the average man that's just not attainable. Some of us gain muscle just by looking at a weight rack whilst others are so called "hard gainers".

Among other concerns for men are hair loss, height, and skin care. The hair loss industry is estimated to be worth over a billion dollars. There is so much stigma around the subject. Men feel less attractive and have significant anxiety about it with linked feelings of inadequacy and low self-esteem. In recent years male skin care has become another major industry with so many male specific skin care brands out there marketing their products. Plus male cosmetic procedures are increasing every year including procedures such as liposuction, facial surgery and even male breast reduction being some of the most popular.

Generally most men report to being happy with the procedures but there are some that are never satisfied with the results of cosmetic interventions. In those cases they are likely to be suffering from a psychiatric disorder called body dysmorphic disorder (BDD).
According to research by Mayo Clinic over two percent of men have BDD. This is defined as a chronic mental illness manifesting in a person constantly thinking about flaws in their appearance. Amogst the men who suffer from BDD suicide attempts are even more common. That flare could be real, imagined or minor. For some men it can be that they are already so ripped and muscular yet they still feel scrawny. For most men it is completely undiagnosed and remains there blocking them from living their best life.

In cases with BDD the patients are so focused and preoccupied with relatively small or in some cases absent deformity that causes significant distress to their mental wellbeing. Usually they obsess about this perceived disorder and are consumed by it. For someone considering cosmetic surgery it is important to recognize BDD. In fact before considering any cosmetic surgery seek a trained psychologist's advice to determine if your reasons for the surgery are valid. They will assess your psychiatric history and current mental state. If you have heightened psychiatric conditions then psychiatric treatment would be more beneficial because in the case of BDD people are rarely going to see any long term benefits from cosmetic surgery.

Managing body image issues

Body image issues are certain to have compounded during your lifetime and so to change them into something more positive will take some time. Start with reflecting back on your childhood and identifying the things that might have caused your poor body image. Maybe you were picked on for being too small or maybe you always wanted to look like your favorite movie star. Whatever it is from now on let go of it and promise yourself to treat your body with more respect. This includes not just the way you think about your body but also what you put into it and how you treat it. Consider all of the things that your body can do besides just how it looks. Sure the big guys look great but can they outrun you? Most of those big bodybuilders will be gassed out after just a short jog. Focus on longevity and exercising for feeling better instead of looking better. Stop all of the body-checking, pinching, measuring and comparing yourself.

Accept your body for what it is. Be happy with how you look and stop being desperate to fix it because society pressures you to look a certain way. Shut that noise out and block any sites or social media that push those ideals in your face. Curate a more positive feed into your life. Get involved with other male friends and talk about body image issues with them. Don't be afraid of vulnerability and being open about your issues. That is how you can heal. Overall embrace your body and be happy with the way you look. If you're out of shape then focus on practicing better exercise and healthier diet habits. It's natural to feel insecure now and again. In the long run be kind to yourself and develop more positive and healthy habits.

Performance anxiety and sexual dysfunction

Another particularly sensitive area for men is in the bedroom. Masculine social conditioning, pornography and toxic masculinity have all added pressure to men having to perform well in the bedroom. In fact it is all too common for men of all ages to at some point experience performance anxiety and or erectile dysfunction (ED).

Expectations are placed on a man often by himself to put on a great performance. This is all bad and often negatively affects ED and performance. Then worse still if these expectations are not met it leads to a downward spiral. Negative thinking about one's abilities in the bedroom lead to performance anxiety and can also cause ED. Maybe it's a fear about sexual inadequacy or the fear of not being enough for their partner. Those feelings can come about because of body image issues or because of their false perception of what it means to be a man in the bedroom. Maybe they feel they have to be her "best lover" or to put on "the best performance".

Research has concluded that there is a clear connection between a man's state of mind and his sexual performance. The biggest causes are stress and anxiety. In addition more general negative thoughts, low self-esteem and stress can also contribute. On a serious note it can be an actual body issue related to nerves or blood circulation. If the symptoms persist after your mental issues have been resolved then seek medical help.

Overcoming performance anxiety and ED can be achieved in a number of ways. All of which can lead to much more positive and fulfilling sexual experiences for both partners. If it is an ongoing issue with your partner then first of all break the cycle. Should you find yourself dwelling on issues, comparisons, past experiences and so on instead shift your focus to what the source of the issue is. Maybe you have some project at work that is stressing you out or an upcoming family event. Shift the focus to the cause rather than the symptoms and it may help to reduce the pressure to perform. Work on improving it with your partner and build more intimacy through communication and being vulnerable.

Focus on your senses. During and before sexual activity many men worry about what their sexual partner is thinking or about how they will be perceived. Instead focus your mind on the senses. Focus on what your hands feel, the touch of your skin on eachothers, what your eyes are seeing and so on. Be completely in the moment. To help you, use some scented candles and music to stir the senses.

Finally make sure you get regular exercise. Not only will this help to reduce stress and anxiety it will also increase your testosterone. A simple thirty minute exercise routine a few times a week will produce results. Try performing kettlebell and pelvic exercises to build stronger erections. In addition practice meditation or therapy with your partner.

Exercise

Become more physically active. This is great not just for your health and body image but also for your self-esteem. When you're more comfortable in your own body naturally it will create a better self-esteem.

Find some activities to help you get fit. That could be anything from joining a walking group to playing tennis. Aim to exercise everyday even if it's just for thirty minutes. In addition try to eat more healthy. Avoid the quick fix junk food and replace it with some fruit or fresh salads.

Confidence in Conversation and Socializing

Making friends and going out to socialize can feel risky particularly if you're suffering from low self-esteem and confidence issues. Social gatherings and meeting people becomes much more difficult. The fear of rejection or judgement is so strong that those suffering neglect to express their true ideas and personality. But through developing our social skills it can help to raise our self-esteem and confidence. Much like other skills socializing becomes better the more you practice it.

Start with finding some social activities in your local area. Go alone if possible, otherwise you will be more likely to stick to your friends all the time. Going alone will encourage you to talk with new people and in turn build your social confidence. Make yourself more accountable for going out. Set appointments and stick to them. Go out there, take risks and resist the urge to cancel any social event. It can be easy and tempting to back out of a social event. Maybe it seems like you have a valid excuse but ultimately it's best that you do go out there. The more you avoid taking action the easier it becomes to isolate yourself and reinforce any avoidance behaviour.

Social skills & better conversations

When you're out gaining social experience practice confident behaviour. Project confident body language. Focus on having good eye contact, posture and clear, audible speaking. Remember to stay calm and breathe deeply if you start to get stressed. It's all about the process more so than the results. Don't depend on any external gratification instead focus on being social and enjoying the moment.

People are attracted to familiarity and when they see people who are like themselves they are more likely to warm to them. Practice mirroring the body language of the people you speak with. Mirror their tone, speed, volume and gestures. But don't be too obvious about it. Do it in a subtle way to gain better rapport with them. For example if they use certain words you can use similar ones. Or if they are facing a certain way then do the same. But again be subtle.

Be sure to smile. A slow smile that takes longer to emerge is usually rated as being more charming and authentic. Smile with your whole face. In fact have a light smile the whole time you're out and then during the moments where you need to smile more use a full face smile. Not only will this make others feel better around you it will also make you feel happier.

Have some conversation starters prepared in your head or written down. Rehearse some introductory lines or when in doubt ask people to talk about themselves. For example, "How do you know the host?" or "What brought you here?" By default many of us panic about running out of things to say. We are not able to get past the pleasantries and get into a real conversation. To counter this come prepared with a handful of subjects that you feel comfortable to talk about. That could be things such as the local city, the subject of the event itself, a current business trend or even a movie you recently saw.

Take things deeper and go beyond the small talk. At the start of a conversation some small talk is necessary but maybe there is someone whom you really want to connect with. In that case try to find a common thread that connects you both. Maybe it's someone you both know, something you both have experienced or a place you've both been too. Find out what motivates them and they will want to share more deeply with you. Encourage this discovery by showing interest in what they say and by asking for more information. Give them your full attention and it will bring about wonderful conversations.

When it's your time to speak, tell stories to captivate people. Stories are great because they can display your strengths and authenticity in a practical way. You can have some go to stories prepared. Make sure your stories show you in a positive way and are something relatable. Usually something with humour and that shows you overcame some challenge works well. Stay humble.

Start conversations on a positive note and try to maintain that positive vibe. Avoid negative subjects such as the weather, politics or bad news. It's better to be more positive with new people. If the conversation veers negative try and steer it back or reframe it to the positive. Always end on a positive note also. When it comes time to say goodbye, say something positive, such as 'I really enjoyed talking with you,' or 'I love your style by the way.' When people reflect on their conversations with you it will be in a positive light.

Commit to speaking to at least three new people. Going to an event and just talking to one person or sticking to your friend isn't going to help you to improve your social skills much. Now you don't need to go out and talk to every single person. Instead set a realistic and valuable goal. Aim to introduce yourself and have a conversation with three new people. If that's too much then just go for two and then work from there. Always try to push yourself a little bit more each time and break through the walls of comfort. Maybe that's talking to a person for longer or to more new people.

It's important to note here that you should not rely on any stimulants to boost your confidence. If there is alcohol involved and you're going to drink then do so in moderation. A little will be fine but don't rely on it. After the event go home and reflect on the experience. Take into account things you need to improve on or do more of.

Eliminate the fear of rejection

Are you convinced that people won't accept your opinions? Are you convinced that people won't approve of your looks, values or beliefs? These fears of rejection are all irrational and they can significantly diminish your daily life choices and actions. Under the influence of fear of rejection your career prospects, relationships and social interactions are all negatively affected. Ultimately it is detrimental to the quality of your life. Fear of rejection is holding you back from being yourself.

Part of being human is the longing to be accepted and to be wanted. Out of fear of not having these needs met we withdraw and avoid reaching out. True it hurts to be rejected but it also humbles us and gives us another chance to try again with a stronger foundation. That's if you choose to. When we can notice our inner critic and have awareness for the way we react and encounter fears then we can work towards overcoming them. When we do that we can gain more experience and learn.

The world we live in is very much socially orientated and we are by nature social beings. It's not what you know, it's who you know. Social interactions involve an element of risk of judgment, criticism and rejection. Just as the sun rises each day this is a fact of nature. What people think, do ory say is out of our control. However with more confidence and social intelligence you can reduce the impacts of rejection and be better able to assert yourself. The more competent you become at socializing the more confidence and social intelligence you will develop. In addition others will look up to you for guidance, acceptance and approval.

Think back over your life. Remember a time when you did something brave and daring. All of us have taken a risk and gone for something at least once. If you did it once, then you can do it again and again. Overcome your fear of rejection because it is the greatest obstacle to your success. The antidote is to learn to love yourself. Through developing your courage and self-esteem you can start to break through your fear of rejection. Act courageously in a fearful situation even when you feel the fear.

"Instead of avoiding it, to overcome your fear, I believe you need to embrace it." - Georges St-Pierre (UFC Champion)

Addressing and managing fear takes work and effort. But the results will be worth it because you will gain more freedom. To help you face your fears use the following two step process.

Step one: What do you want?

The first step to overcoming fear of rejection is to identify what you want and why you want it. There need to be real reasons for you to face fear. Without a good reason you will have little motivation. Ask yourself,

- *What do I want?*
- *Why is this important?*
- *How will I benefit?*
- *If I don't take action what will I miss out on?*

The answers to these questions should give you more clarity and in turn a stronger motivation.

Step two: Clarity

In order to overcome any fear you need clarity of the fear. Begin with identifying the thing you fear. Ask yourself,

- *What type of rejection do I fear?*
- *Who do I fear being rejected by?*

- *Why?*

The answers to these questions should give you more clarity about what you fear. Most problems can be solved here by clearly defining what bothers you. But you will still need a little more information about the specific things that happen when you experience this fear. It's time to identify the behaviours that limit you here. Ask yourself when I fear rejection...

- *How do I behave?*
- *How is this hurting me?*

After running through these questions you should by now have significant information about your fear. For best results write out the answers. Next identify more useful behaviors to deal with your fears. Ask yourself the following questions.

- *How else could I approach or think about this situation?*
- *How would this be helpful?*

Finally, define any obstacles that you might need to work through on the way to overcoming your fear of rejection. Ask yourself the following questions.

- *What potential obstacles are there?*
- *What is the worst possible thing that can happen?*
- *Are they real or imagined?*
- *How will I overcome them?*

Obstacles can be real and they can be all in your head. Usually when it comes to the fear of rejection they are mostly in your head. But that's good news because if you take the previous steps then you can challenge and eventually overcome them. In any case resolve to accept the worst possible outcome. Once you are confident that you can accept the worst that could happen write out how you would overcome it and then you no longer need to worry about it. Worry is just an effect of indecision and the only antidote is to take action.

Get busy doing whatever you need to do. Through action your confidence will increase and your fears will begin to disappear. As we grow in confidence through these experiences we start to form better relationships, have a better quality of life and are in turn less intimidated by rejection. In any event that upsets you when you're rejected remember to not take life so seriously and be able to laugh it off. A lighthearted attitude will serve you well in life.

Nervousness and Social Anxiety

Feeling nervous in social situations is completely normal. Maybe you get butterflies before a presentation or before going on a date. All of that is completely human. But when nervousness and anxiety cause you to fear everyday normal situations then it becomes a problem. In severe cases it can dramatically disrupt normal life. If nervousness and social anxiety are affecting your life and causing you to avoid people and social interactions then you need to address the issue. Thankfully there are specific steps that you can take.

Get help

Social anxiety is a real mental health condition and the more you ignore it the harder it becomes to treat. Don't wait or be too ashamed to ask for help from a trained professional. Search for one in your local area.

Journal

Journaling has been proven time and time again to significantly improve mental health. Keep track of your personal interactions and the inner dialogue that comes up during socializing. This will help you to identify stresses, causes and what helps you to feel better. Keep a journal always.

Prioritize

Through prioritizing the time you spend on the things you enjoy you can avoid more of the situations that bring you anxiety. Maybe it's about you spending less time with people who make you feel anxious and spending more time with the people who lift you up. Be conscious of who you're spending time with and how they make you feel. Prioritize the right people, activities and carefully manage your time and energy.

Avoid unhealthy substances

Studies have shown that alcohol, drugs, caffeine and cigarettes can all cause anxiety. If you find yourself dependent on or abusing any of them then take steps to quit. If that's too hard then get help from a Dr, find a treatment program or a support group to help you.

Charisma

Imagine being the charming, intelligent and funny person in the room. Some people just radiate positive energy and effortlessly draw people to them. They have this magnetic charisma. This is the charismatic one and it is one of the most appealing qualities that someone can have. With the power of charisma it will attribute you to have better relationships and more success in life.

Charisma is a combination of confidence and positivity. Charismatic people are able to make people feel comfortable very early on. Simply put it's a kind of personal magnetism. Charisma is often referred to as a trait which is an integral part of the human character. Well this is good news because it means we are all born with it. It's just that the amount of charisma in each of us varies. Everyone can learn to be charismatic in their own way. In order to build charisma you first need to understand exactly what it is.

Becoming charismatic requires self-acceptance, composure and confidence. In other words charismatic people are comfortable with who they are, they remain calm in all situations and they exude confidence. Normally people who want to be charismatic are coming at it from a bad mindset. Many of them believe that they are socially awkward and boring. In reality the root of the problem is a self-image problem combined with an approval-seeking attitude. For them they need to be liked and validated by others. Rejection crushes them and so they try to cover it up by acting charismatic. Only this makes them feel more socially awkward because their behaviour is miscalibrated.

Self-acceptance

When trying to learn charisma the common practice is for people to imitate others. I'm sure you've come across people who try too hard for you to like them. Their attempts come off as insecure and they push people away instead of attracting them. Charisma on the other hand is much more subtle and natural. In turn this makes you even more anxious and you fall into a negative loop.

Becoming charismatic isn't about learning some tricks or copying others. It's simply about not thinking too much about being charismatic and instead learning to like and express yourself more. Each of us has our own natural temperament and strengths. When you attempt to be someone else it will just be weird and unnatural. For you to become a charismatic person you have to match your natural temperament and strengths to your own type of charisma.

First of all you need to improve your self image. Becoming charismatic will be much easier in that regard. If you've followed the advice in this book so far then you have some solid knowledge and strategies to achieve that. To give you a quick run down try the following:

- Acknowledge your qualities

- Ask other people what it is that they like about you
- Assume that others like you
- Reframe negative thoughts about yourself to be more positive
- Accept and embrace rejection
- Follow your passion and do more of what you love

Composure and confidence

Combine these key actions with everything you have learned about confidence and you will be well on your way to being more charismatic in your own way. With an improved self image you will naturally have better composure and confidence as a direct positive consequence. Ultimately this will help you to feel more comfortable in social settings. You will be able to be your own blend of honesty, confidence and authenticity which will be perceived as charismatic. Just like going to the gym the more you work this the more your own blend of charisma develops which is in tune with your natural temperament and strengths.

Masking

Masking is when a person changes their natural personality in order to comply with social pressure, abuse or harassment. This can be strongly influenced by for example dominant parents, rejection or abuse. Sometimes we wear a mask to fit into society's expectations. Maybe that's showing off to your superiors or acting smart to fit in. Often we just want to fit in and be normal. Realize that there is no so-called being normal.

I'm sure all of us have experienced this to an extent before. When we are not being ourselves. We are hiding behind a mask. In some cases this can be effective but when it happens it hurts our chances of real authenticity and confidence. This requires identifying who are your real friends and allies. Are the people you call friends really your friends if they don't know the real you?

Taking this mask and revealing our true selves requires confidence. It is not possible that you're a perfect and flawless person. It's human nature to want to fit in and compare ourselves. Stay true to who you are.

Exercise

Emotions are motions which literally means the way you feel is directly connected to your body movement. Try smiling up to the sky with your arms outstretched. Does that make you feel happier? Of course it does!
Everyday I want you to do some kind of exercise and combine it with asking positive questions of yourself. Write down at least four empowering questions. Google these or come up with your own, for example.

- *What am I happy about?*
- *Who loves me?*
- *What is my favourite memory?*
- *What inspires me?*

As you ask yourself these questions do some light exercise. That could be a walk, stretching or going to the gym. Do this at least once a day.

Work and Relationships

Work

Research by The Harvard Business School found that one of the main reasons that managers did not promote employees was because they didn't appear confident enough. In addition when it comes to applying for jobs many people are much less likely to apply if they are not confident in their abilities for the advertised position.

Instead we need to project confidence and believe that we are ready. After all we can learn a lot on the job. Become comfortable with that idea. True some companies need to be more considerate but it's also true that the world out there is competitive. We live in a capitalist society and so we need to do our best to achieve the success we deserve. To help you become more comfortable and successful at work here are some things you can focus on improving.

Communication Skills

Do you struggle to get your point across and say what you really want to at work? Maybe when you're in a meeting and you want to get your point across but you don't feel comfortable with speaking up. It happens again and again. Then the more you remain passive the bigger the confidence issue becomes.

Communication plays a key role in how you are perceived by your colleagues. A significant part of this is being able to be a good, active listener. When you listen actively to others it shows them that you're involved in the conversation and it stimulates a better interaction. It also helps you to reflect on the right questions to ask and to come up with better ways to communicate your message to them. People will be more warm towards you as a result because you have shown that you understand them. Learn to listen more closely to others and it will position you as an integral part of a team or project.

When you speak, aim to speak with confidence. Remind yourself that your ideas are valuable. For some of you that might seem like a stretch and you would just prefer to stay quiet. Especially in a meeting this can seem even more daunting. The boss asks your opinion and you just nod. Turn it around. Think of someone who you admire. How do they communicate? Are they naturally charismatic, do their words flow? Understand that they probably were not always this way. Most people are not naturally good at speaking, they had to learn the skills.

Practice the skill and face your fears. Toastmasters is an excellent organization that offers public speaking classes in most of the major cities around the world. Memberships costs are low and the benefits far outweigh them. They are dedicated to help people become better at public speaking and grow their leadership skills. Wherever you are, find the nearest Toastmasters club and start learning how to have your voice heard and communicated with ease. Learning to speak more confidently will help you to get your point across.

Finally do your homework and make sure that you always come prepared in advance. This might be obvious advice but failure to be prepared at work in meetings and so on is likely to bring on anxiety. Take a moment before any meeting or work appointment to analyze all that you need to be aware of from any printed materials to agendas and so on. By doing your homework in advance it will give you a better understanding of the scenario and in turn more confidence.

Naturally your confidence at work will go through peaks and dips. Sometimes you might be in a bad work situation and it affects your confidence. But if you keep working at it your base level of confidence will keep rising and the challenges will be easier to overcome.

People pleasing

People pleasing is an easy activity for anyone to get caught up in. People usually default it because they have been conditioned to think that they must do so in order to be seen as a "good person". In addition, low self-esteem may also cause people to engage in pleasing people. Ultimately it comes down to not approving of yourself.

Men in particular from a young age are conditioned to seek approval from women. They had to "be a good boy" and sit still for mommy. Then we had to make a good impression on our school crushes. It all feeds into making men pursuers with an ongoing seeking to get that stamp of approval from women. Men will buy silly clothes, waste money and do all kinds of things to try to seek attention and validation from women. But women don't respect this kind of behaviour because it's not authentic. Additionally our parents wanted the best from us. Sometimes they wanted something different for us than what we wanted. Maybe they wanted you to become a Dr or a lawyer. Whilst you wanted to be an artist or astronaut.

Fundamentally all of us want to be liked and to be accepted. Evolution wired us to be this way. Every time you do something that will ensure or promote your survival your brain releases dopamine. For example, when you eat, have sex, take drugs or spend money your brain releases dopamine. Around the world millions of people are addicted to these destructive habits. But they aren't addicted to the actual food, drugs, sex or spending cash. No instead what causes the addiction is the dopamine release linked to them. When you get that hit of dopamine it's a sign you're doing something right and you are validated in the moment.

In the present world social media is another culprit of this addictive validation seeking behaviour and it takes it to a whole new level. The likes, comments and interaction all give us dopamine hits which is addictive. It's all too easy to live a passive life and to not actually gain any real value in your life. Why go out and meet new people when you can sit on your couch and get validation? The desire for validation quickly forms a bad habit. Soon enough you need more likes and comments. But if you get less it makes you sad.

At the end of a day you're living a life that it is not yours. In effect you're a slave. Yes we all want recognition on some level and people want to know that they matter. A little bit of that is fine because we need to have recognition to achieve success. The problem is that too many people are desperately seeking attention and approval that they will sacrifice their integrity. They will do things such as suck up to the boss or post overly emotional, provocative pictures online. All of that is no good because if you're constantly chasing other people's attention it's like chasing the wind and you will have no peace.

Understand that your life is in your hands. The desire to please people is based on outside sources. The world outside of us is out of our control and whenever we reach for controlling it that can set us up for disappointment. We expect things to go a certain way or people to behave a certain way and when those expectations don't match reality disappointment sets in. Then we lack the courage to take a chance doing something we want to do or to live the life we really want. We want popularity, social status and validation at the jeopardy of our own happiness.

Now you might be thinking. But I want to get ahead and fit in with society, so why not seek approval? Well the price comes that we only get approval from others at the expense of our own true desires. In effect we miss out on our own self approval and that holds us back from being true to yourself. In fact through seeking the approval of others you are negatively impacting your effectiveness. It starts with avoiding doing things which are important to you or trying anything that makes you feel anxious or is out of your comfort zone. For example you know you want to talk to that woman but you fear people shaming you. Or you want to talk with your boss about a better deal but you don't want him to hate you for speaking up. Essentially your need for approval leads to countless lost opportunities and more often than not you will give up before even starting out. With deep self love we can be comfortable who we are regardless of external approval or circumstance. Be happy and live your life because life's too short to be anything else.

"It always seems impossible until it's done." - Nelson mandela

How is your need for approval holding you back? Maybe as a high achiever you try your best to make others happy. But it leaves you feeling overwhelmed and never free to do what you want. If this is relatable to you and you're finding yourself hurt by it then it's time for you to make a change. When you identify this and move past it you can be free to go for what you really want. Fundamentally this requires knowing who you are. Ask yourself what you value and what do you want to spend your time doing. You should be aligned with your own goals and values. Success is measured by doing more of what matters to you.

"Success is doing what you want to do, when you want, where you want, with whom you want, as much as you want." - Tony Robbins

Begin to become more self aware and authentic regardless of peoples reactions. When people ask something of you take the time to evaluate whether it's right for you and be honest with them. Take note of the things you're doing and whether or not they are to seek approval or people please. If they are approval seeking activities then stop.

Practice saying no. You can still be kind and polite, yet definitive. For example "I would love to do that but I really have something important already planned, but thank you anyway." In this way you will find that most people will respect you for your politeness and for standing your ground. Anything you do should not be at the sake of your happiness and someone else's. If it makes you unhappy don't do it. In some cases yes short term suffering is fine but long term you don't want to be exploited. The choice is yours.

Taking a step away and shutting out certain activities or people is an effective way to break an addiction to validation. Recognize any codependency issues. Essentially this is a dysfunctional, relationship in which one person requires the other to fulfill their emotional needs. On a small scale its little hits of dopamine such as them texting you back. On a larger scale it turns into obsessive behaviour. If there's someone in your life triggering this behaviour in you then you need to be brave and cut them out. Maybe it's an ex partner or an estranged family member. If you follow someone online and they cause this emotional state in you then simply block them and shut it out.

Making habits harder to happen is effective. Maybe you stop hanging out with certain people, move away or close social media accounts. At first withdrawal will make you crave that validation even more. But this is the hard part where you need to stand your ground and not give in. Make it really hard for you to do that habit. For example if you like to get high, block your dealers number and move away. Or if social media is a problem then uninstall apps, block sites and turn off the wifi. By the time you have started to try and engage in those validation activities your self discipline will have kicked in.

Assertiveness

Assertiveness training is a method of helping people get what they want in a skilful and practical way without sacrificing their relationships. Cure the disease to please. Essentially being assertive is about standing up for who you are, what you believe in and standing by your values. When you believe something is the right thing to do, you do it regardless of pressure from others.

People who are naturally assertive usually have strong confidence. But people who suffer from low self-esteem often struggle to ask for what they want. They default to being quiet and not letting their true feelings known. As a result their confidence diminishes and they get what life gives them which isn't always what they want. Practice being assertive. State your opinions, take the lead and if you don't want to do something then speak out.

Speaking up for what we want and for who we are is crucial to healthy self-esteem and confidence. The inability to assert yourself comes from fear and irrational belief systems. When we fail to assert ourselves it sends a message that we are not enough and it is enforced the more we fail to do so. People are likely to take advantage of us. Additionally the retreat into silence harbours feelings of frustration which eventually builds into resentment or worse can even boil over into anger. Maybe on some level we fear hurting others or we are afraid of being perceived in the wrong way. Because of this we avoid making any requests and prefer to stay quietly uncomfortable. In the worst case we hold others above us, shut down and become passive.

Taking care of our needs and being empowered comes from asserting yourself in the world around you. Direct and affirmative action and communication promotes better relationships. We stay true to ourselves, act in our best interests and express who we are. This helps to establish healthy boundaries and improves the chances that we fulfill our needs and goals. Ultimately it builds and maintains a healthy level of self-esteem.

Life will always present situations where even being assertive doesn't always meet your needs and goals. It's true life can be challenging and you will encounter difficult people who don't regard healthy communication as being important. But don't let any of that discourage you from speaking up, respecting and asserting yourself. Incidentally try not to be overly assertive. That's just arrogance. Strike a healthy balance, never be a victim and never be a bully. With practice and persistence you can build a healthy amount of assertiveness and in turn self-esteem which will enhance your life experience.

Dating and positive relationships

Advice for singles

All of us have had that feeling of meeting or seeing someone attractive who makes our heart beat a little faster. Maybe it's that lady you see at the coffee shop every morning or the local waitress. But you never have the courage to go talk with her. Your self-esteem is holding you back and you're also making up excuses for things that didn't even happen yet.

Reality is what is out there in the world. You might think someone will react a certain way or you might predict some outcome but the fact is you don't know until you try. Yes you might be afraid of how they respond or if the people around will judge you. But really do you have anything to lose? Or do you have more to gain? Maybe you just say hi and they don't say much back. But then you've overcome your self-esteem issues and built your confidence in doing so. Or maybe you say hi and it starts a great conversation which leads to much more. Taking action is the ultimate antidote. Otherwise that opportunity might never come again.

Everyday try to break through your comfort zone. Become comfortable talking with strangers and the other sex. Say hi to people you come across. Next time someone gets in the elevator with you or catches your eye there is your chance. Be in the moment and keep engaging with the world around you. As an effect of this more social behaviour you will become more attractive and smoother with the people you are attracted to. Keep going.

Better relationships and love

According to research on more than five hundred men and women conducted by The Journal of Personality and Social Psychology, low self-esteem can create a negative perception of your partner. People with low self-esteem are much more likely to feel inferior and have a negative focus on their relationships. Understandably this can be tough. It can lead to insecurity, anxiety and overall frustration from both sides. Ultimately it makes the relationship unstable. The key to dealing with this is to notice any negative self talk and to address it. Use the advice and exercises in this book.

Healthy self-esteem is essential for healthy relationships. The amount you can love someone else depends on how much you love yourself. If your inner dialogue is negative and self-deprecating then you need to work on it using the advice in this book. Train yourself to be a more positive person and with practice it will grow your relationship into a much more loving one. If you feel not good about yourself then you will never be able to let someone else love you. A poor sense of self worth will trap you in bad relationships and sabotage the good ones.

Now having high self-esteem doesn't necessarily mean you will have a happy relationship. However it will give you the self actualization to identify what you truly want and help to make sure you get what you deserve. It will also give you the courage to walk away from a bad relationship. If that's the case then acknowledge it and do something about it. Here are a few suggestions for increasing the positivity in your relationships.

Avoid criticizing, blaming, and shaming

Excessive judgement and criticism are usually the sign of an unhealthy relationship which eventually leads to feelings of shame. Unfortunately many couples fall into habits of arguing and criticizing each other. These attacks on each other are likely to cause feelings of shame or embarrassment and might even reignite wounds from the past. Next time you feel angry at your partner take a moment to consider your comments and the effect that they will have. Consistent criticism will ultimately deteriorate a relationship.

Accept each other

Falling in love and being in a relationship is based on loving each other for who they are. No one is perfect. Accept each other's mistakes as part of their humanity. Learn to appreciate your partner. Praise them for the things you value about them. Open your heart for them to confide in and trust in you. Speak genuine words to them. That doesn't mean being all fluffy, sometimes your partner will just need an ear to listen, a shoulder to cry on or some genuine feedback.

As a product of accepting each other you will have a much more loving and deep relationship. If you are in a relationship with someone who you love and value then there is an opportunity for you to both grow. How you communicate with each other will either have a positive or negative impact on both of your self-esteem.

Criticism (and how to respond to it)

Let's face it you're never going to escape criticism in life. Especially at work and in your relationships. How you respond to it will ultimately affect your long term self-esteem. Your response will determine whether the criticism about you is taken as a positive chance to improve or as a negative attack on your self-esteem.

As humans we are all imperfectly perfect and so criticism will always be inevitable. But we need to take it as an opportunity to learn and improve. Often we struggle to look at ourselves objectively. Take a step back and try to see things from the other person's point. We can all learn from our mistakes by dealing with criticism positively and in a mature way. Being able to practice this is a sign of strong emotional intelligence and high self-esteem. Criticism can be categorized as either irrelevant, destructive, or constructive.

Irrelevant criticism

This kind of criticism is best to be ignored. Usually it comes from the kind of people who are critical of everything and everyone. Typically they will throw in criticism that has nothing to do with the situation at hand. Of course it's natural to feel some kind of emotion towards criticism but take a second to assess if it is really relevant or worthy of a response. Usually it is not worth responding to or getting emotional about

Destructive criticism

This kind of criticism is a form of attack on someone's character. Should you be on the receiving end of this, try to remain calm. Usually there is something wrong with anyone who tries to put down another person. Don't take it personally. Rational and grounded people don't engage in mudslinging. Taking their comments to heart would be a mistake. Instead give them the opportunity to assess what they are saying and question why they would say something so hurtful.

It was once said that a man was abusing Buddha who remained indifferent. This made the man angrier. He shouted "How can you be so calm when I abuse you?" The Buddha remained silent which made the man even more angry. The man shouted again "how can you remain so tranquil?". In response Budhha calmly replied 'If you offered me food, and I refused to eat it, the food remains yours.'

"Nobody can make you feel inferior without your consent" – Eleanor Roosevelt.

Constructive criticism

This kind of criticism is positive and is what you should attribute value to. But some people might take it the wrong way. Don't be one of them. When criticism comes from a place of sincerity or from someone that has your best interests at heart then stay humble and listen. Never respond with anger because this will only create bad feelings. Stay calm and be grateful that you have well intentioned people willing to guide you. Ultimately this kind of criticism will reveal your flaws and help you grow into a more confident person. A real friend or lover will tell you the truth even if it hurts because it contains your best intentions at heart.

Exercise

Practice becoming more assertive
- Attend some toastmasters classes in your local area.
- Write down things you will no longer accept at work. Find solutions to them and take action.

If your single
- Talk to three strangers a day for the next ten days. It could be a simple "hi" to the cashier at the supermarket. Take note of it because what you measure grows.

If your in a relationship
- Open the pathway to a more honest relationship. Practice recognizing when your partner does something nice and return this by doing something nice for them.
- If you're unhappy in your relationship, write down why. Find solutions, be brave and take actions to solve the problem.

Conclusion- Live Life To The Max!

Here we are at the conclusion of our journey towards having more self-esteem and confidence. Congratulations on making it here! It takes courage to be able to recognize your flaws and to recognize an opportunity to improve yourself. I encourage you to all re-read this book more than once. I also encourage you to take the time to do all of the exercises in it. Now let's take a moment to summarize and conclude the most important messages of this book.

In the first chapter we discussed what exactly self-esteem and confidence are. In summary, self-esteem is about how you feel about yourself. It is at the root of confidence which is about your beliefs in your skills and abilities. In that chapter we understood that low levels of self-esteem will hinder your progress in life. Low self-esteem will cause you to over analyze situations, what people think about you and ultimately stop you from living your best life. Confidence is essential to becoming your best self. But remember to display it with grace so as to avoid being perceived as arrogant.

Moving on I detailed the causes of low self-esteem issues. These are really important to be aware of because they are things that we can actually do something about. Everyday we can be affected by any of these factors. One of the biggest causes of low self-esteem issues are negative childhood and life experiences. So if you're a parent remember that you need to strike a good balance of praise and protection to make sure that your children are raised with healthy levels of self-esteem. If you were a victim of past abuse or any of the other causes then remember that it is in the past. Try to let go of that past. You can't control it. But you can take responsibility and control what happens from now on.

Blaming other people will only take you so far. If you have genetic, mental health or other shortcomings then believe that there are still things you can do to counteract them. Try new things, be active and take pride in who you are. Stay healthy and keep in contact with your community. Don't live your life in fear or be stuck being a victim forever. If you need to ask for help then ask. Take the focus off yourself and focus on the solutions.

Isolation and avoidance can be an easy way out. But the more time you spend in avoidance the worse things will get. Get comfortable with the unknown. Keep being out there as much as you can in the world. I know that's difficult right now but this shall all pass. You can still engage with people online and talk about how you feel. Expose yourself to things that make you uncomfortable because those experiences will help you to grow into becoming a stronger person. No one is perfect so you don't need to fear being perceived as not enough. That's just a flawed way of thinking. Value who you are and be grateful for your life. That will give you much longer lasting self confidence and comfort with yourself even if you're not a perfect person.

If you're surrounded by the wrong people then you need to set some boundaries and strive for a better situation. Stand up for yourself, if someone does you wrong to you then call them out on it. If people criticize who you are, learn to respond to them and realize that criticism is a fact of life. If you're falling into bad habits such as excess alcohol, drugs or addictive behaviours then realise that the more you engage these behaviors the worse they will spiral into lower self esteem. Practice mindfulness and accountability for your actions. There are other ways to deal with low self-esteem than these destructive behaviours. Replace them with things that make you feel good and that also develop some skills. That could be things like cooking, going to the gym or enjoying the simple pleasures of life. Essentially they should improve your life and have a positive consequence.

Later on in the book I talked about accessing your inner voice and becoming aware of any negative thoughts and beliefs. Beliefs are at the core of who you are. Negative beliefs can cause psychological problems and low self-esteem. Follow the advice in this book to become aware of your negative thoughts and beliefs. Constantly challenge and replace them with more positive ones.

In addition I talked about retrainining your brain and the language you use. We use language and metaphor to express our emotions in life. Most of this is habitual. With regular practice of using more empowering language the bigger the change in your emotional state will be. The brain will form stronger habitual pathways and you can become a more positive person. Change your language and you change your life

Success is an average of possibilities. The more things you try the higher your chances of success will be. If you can shift your mental state to a higher level then you're going to be more resilient to life challenges and rise above them. When you face those big goals you will be better able to go after them and ignore any negative inner voice.

    An important part of this book was about sharing and being vulnerable. Society forces false realities and pressures for us to live up to. We are living in approval for others at the sake of our own emotions. There are too many false constructions out there about what it means to be a man. Contrary to popular belief it's not about being some big alpha, muscle guy. The truth is that if you accept yourself as a man then you are well on the way to being the best you can be. Be your own best friend and be authentic.

In order to accept yourself it means loving yourself and until you can really love yourself you can never truly begin to love someone else. That means accepting all of you, particularly your body image which is such a big factor towards people's negative thinking. Body issues can consume thoughts and diminish a person's ability just to enjoy a simple life. Performance and sexual dysfunction is another area of sensitivity for men. Negative thinking can also impact on the ability for a man to perform in the bedroom. Shift the focus to the cause rather than the symptoms. Focus on your senses and being completely in the moment.

Most body issues again come down to comparing ourselves against false constructs such as comparing to ripped actors or models. These people are hiring teams of nutritionists and personal trainers. Plus they are brushing things up in editing software. For the average person that's just not attainable. Focus on being you and taking good care of yourself. Only compare yourself to who used to be and to who you are right now. Now it's not something that is going to happen overnight. It will take a lot of work because you're going to have to overcome many mental hurdles, but stick with it.

Finally we talked about socialising, workplace and relationships confidence. Making friends is a risky endeavor because rejection and judgement is such a feared thing. Through taking responsibility for improving your social skills and going out there it's going to contribute to you having higher self-esteem. All of this will keep compounding with practice.

We all fear rejection because we want to be accepted. Yes, when we get rejected it does hurt but it also humbles us and gives us a lesson or chance to grow. Addressing the fear of rejection requires work after but if you use the steps in this book then you will be able to much better deal with it when it happens. Plus you won't be stuck in any bad habits of pleasing people behaviours because you'll be more self-aware and more fearless. As a positive side effect you will become more charismatic and if you follow the steps in that chapter it will influence you to have better relationships and success in your life. You will be comfortable to stand up to your boss and assert yourself in the workplace. Keep working on your communication skills and being a good listener. When you speak, do it with confidence.

Healthy self-esteem is also essential for healthy relationships. When it comes to dating if you're single you need to to stop making up false scenarios in your head as to why you think someone is going to reject you. The reality is what's out there, every day keep breaking through your comfort zone and engage with the world. Now if you're in a relationship again realise that self-esteem is critical for healthy relationships. Love and accept your partner for who they are. Set boundaries for what you will and won't accept. Avoid any criticism, blame or shame.

Ok so now for the most important message of this book. Accept yourself so you can feel good about yourself. Ultimately you need to believe in yourself and have complete faith in yourself. Remember that I said if you've had bad stuff happen to you in the past, realize that you can't control it but you can control who you're going to be today. Blaming others will only take you so far. Take full responsibility for your life and make yourself feel like you matter in this world.

Understand that you are not your thoughts and they don't rule who you are. You can change them and make them more empowering. Once you do that your life will start to improve. That might sound easier said than done but when you apply just a little bit of effort to become more positive in your thoughts everyday it starts to compound. It's your life and no one else's. Yes it will take some work to create a healthy sense of self-esteem and it begins with taking full responsibility for your life.

Always keep moving forward towards your success and challenging yourself to be more comfortable with the uncomfortable. It's a journey, your self-esteem and confidence will fluctuate each day. You're going to have bad days and you're going to have good days. But the more you can raise your general level of self-esteem and confidence then the better you can become.

If you're doing more of what you love and doing less of what you hate. Plus mixing it with authenticity and awareness of your internal dialogue then you can become more detached from the negative self talk. Ultimately that will help you to realise who you are and make that mental shift towards building your self-esteem and confidence.

Make yourself matter in this world and be your own best friend.

Thanks for Reading!

I know you could have picked any number of books to read, but you picked this book and for that I am extremely grateful.

To help me become a better writer, to stay motivated and to hear back from you please leave an honest review of this book at the place of where you purchased it. I want you to know that I read these reviews and am grateful for them. They encourage me to write and to improve.

I would really appreciate your feedback and questions. You can keep in touch with me at:

www.darcycarter.com

chaseattraction@gmail.com

Thank you and all the best to you.

Darcy Carter

The First 9 Things A Woman Notices

Free Cheat Sheet For Attracting Women

Click Here

Click Here

Resources

Offline

Henry David Thoreau (1854). *Walden*. Ticknor and Fields: Boston

Gautama Buddha. *The Dhammapada (Quote)*

Sylvestor Stallone (2006). *Rocky Balboa (film)*. MGM Distribution Co.

Arnold Schwarzenegger. *(Quote)*.

Albert Bandura (1997). *Self-Efficacy*. W. H. Freeman.

John B. Watson (est 1960). *Cognitive Behavioral Therapy.*

Carl R. Rogers (1995). *On Becoming a Person: A Therapist's View of Psychotherapy.* Houghton Mifflin

Daniel Craig (James Bond), (2006). *Casino Royale (film).* Sony Pictures.

Vivien Leigh (Scarlett), Clark Gable (Rhett), (1939). *Gone with the Wind (film).* Loew's Inc.

Bruce Lee. *(Quote)*.

Body Image (2016). *Body Image - An International Journal of Research.* Editor-in-Chief: Tracy L. Tylka.

Georges St-Pierre. *(Quote)*.

The Harvard Business School (2011). *How to Build Confidence - Harvard Business Review 2011.* The Harvard Business School.

Nelson Mandela. *(Quote)*.

Tony Robbins. *(Quote)*.

Eleanor Roosevelt (2004). *Free, Fearless, Female: Wild Thoughts on Womanhood.* Willow Creek Press. Minocqua, Wisconsin.

Online

European Social Survey - *Prospectus European Social Survey European Research Infrastructure Consortium.* (2010) https://www.europeansocialsurvey.org/

The National Health Service (NHS) - *Suicide Factsheet.* (2005) https://www.swlstg.nhs.uk/

Printed in Great Britain
by Amazon